Abstract Art Revolution

Abstract Art Revolution

NEW STRATEGIES FOR CREATING INNOVATIVE SPACES

Evan Stuart Marshall

ESM Productions

ESM Productions
1 Pacio Court
Roseland, NJ 07068-1121

Printed in the United States of America

ISBN 979-8-218-25712-5 (paperback)
ISBN 979-8-218-25713-2 (ebook)

Contents

Introduction

Welcome to *Abstract Art Revolution*, a guide to transforming spaces using the power of abstract art. Whether in your home, office, or outdoor environments, abstract art holds the potential to elevate and energize any space. It transcends mere decoration—abstract art has the unique ability to evoke emotions, inspire creativity, and spark meaningful conversations.

In this book, we will explore innovative strategies to integrate abstract art into a variety of settings, highlighting its psychological impact and practical benefits. From creating conversation starters to boosting productivity, from nurturing the soul to enhancing the aesthetics and functionality of your environment, abstract art can profoundly shape how we experience and interact with the spaces around us.

Each chapter delves into a different aspect of how abstract art can be utilized, offering fresh and unexpected approaches that push the boundaries of traditional design. Whether you're an art enthusiast, an interior designer, or someone simply looking to add a touch of creativity to your surroundings, this book is your guide to unlocking the transformative power of abstract art.

Let's embark on this creative journey together, discovering how abstract art can not only beautify your spaces but also enrich your everyday experiences.

1

Psychological Dimensions

Abstract art transcends mere aesthetics; it has the potential to serve as a powerful, transformative force in your surroundings, elevating the ambiance of your home or office. In this chapter, we embark on an in-depth exploration of how abstract art—through its unique interplay of color, form, and texture—can metamorphose your environment into a haven of creativity, inspiration, and emotional resonance.

Mood Enhancement: The Emotional Canvas

Abstract art, with its enigmatic and fluid forms, has an incredible ability to influence emotions and shape the mood of a space. By tapping into the language of color and form, abstract art communicates on a visceral level, unlocking emotional responses that subtly but profoundly affect the atmosphere of your surroundings. Whether you're seeking to energize a workspace, create a serene retreat, or stimulate creative thinking, abstract art is the ideal medium for cultivating the desired emotional landscape.

Colors: The Vibrant Palette of Emotion

Imagine a world devoid of color or shape—it would be lifeless, stripped of expression and emotion. Abstract art offers a dynamic channel to convey feelings, thoughts, and ideas through color and form. Let's explore how specific colors have the power to evoke a broad spectrum of emotions, transforming the spaces they occupy into energetic, calming, or creatively stimulating environments.

- **Vibrant Energy**: Bold colors like fiery reds, electric blues, and vivid yellows infuse spaces with vitality and intensity. These hues thrive in areas where creativity, innovation, and passion are at the forefront, making them ideal for spaces like home offices, studios, or workspaces where energy and drive are essential.

  Example: Picture a striking red abstract art piece displayed in your home office. This dynamic work not only enhances the aesthetic of the space but serves as a daily motivator, sparking creativity and fueling enthusiasm for your projects.

- **Serene Calm**: Soft pastels, cool blues reminiscent of tranquil waters, and gentle, flowing shapes create a sense of serenity and relaxation. These colors and forms are perfect for spaces where peace and calm are desired, such as bedrooms, meditation rooms, or reading nooks.

Example: Imagine a large, calming blue abstract painting gracing the wall of your bedroom. The gentle hues work in harmony to foster restful sleep and peaceful mornings, transforming your personal space into a sanctuary of tranquility.

The Psychological Power of Color and Form in Abstract Art

The interplay of color and form in abstract art creates more than just a visual experience—it impacts the mind and emotions in meaningful ways. Understanding the psychology of color and form allows you to intentionally select pieces that align with the mood and atmosphere you want to cultivate in your space.

- **Red**: A color of intensity and excitement, red ignites passion and energy. It's perfect for spaces where dynamic, bold actions are required.

  Example: In a bustling kitchen or collaborative workspace, a large red abstract piece commands attention and inspires creativity and action, making it the ideal backdrop for passionate discussions or brainstorming sessions.

- **Blue**: Known for its calming, soothing qualities, blue is associated with relaxation, tranquility, and mental clarity. Incorporating blue tones into your environment can help cultivate a peaceful, reflective mood.

  Example: A soothing blue abstract work in a meditation space allows individuals to unwind and connect with inner peace, making it a visual anchor for mindfulness practices.

- **Yellow**: Bright and optimistic, yellow evokes happiness, creativity, and a sense of warmth. It is perfect for areas that need a boost of positive energy.

  Example: A workspace illuminated by the bright tones of yellow abstract art fosters a cheerful atmosphere, promoting positivity and enhancing creative thought processes.

- **Green**: Symbolizing balance, growth, and renewal, green abstract art is a calming yet invigorating choice. It brings the vitality of nature into your space.

  Example: Placing green abstract art in a home office or study room fosters a sense of balance, enhancing productivity while maintaining a calming influence.

Shapes and Emotions: The Dance of Form

In addition to color, the shapes and forms in abstract art play a crucial role in influencing emotions and the overall ambiance of a space.

- **Geometric Shapes**: Precise lines and sharp angles evoke a sense of order, structure, and focus. These shapes are ideal for spaces where concentration and productivity are key.

  Example: In a corporate office, abstract art with bold geometric patterns creates a structured environment, enhancing productivity and inspiring innovative solutions among employees.

- **Organic Shapes**: Fluid, free-flowing shapes are associated with comfort, ease, and relaxation. These forms create an inviting, relaxed atmosphere, making them perfect for social spaces like living rooms and lounges.

  Example: In a cozy living room, abstract art with soft, organic curves fosters a sense of warmth and connection, making the space a welcoming environment for family and friends.

The Emotional Impact of Texture in Abstract Art

While color and shape are integral components of abstract art, texture also plays a pivotal role in shaping the emotional tone of a space. Texture adds depth and dimension, influencing how a piece of art is perceived on both visual and tactile levels.

- **Bold, Rough Textures**: A textured surface can evoke intensity and movement. Rough, bold textures in abstract art can bring a sense of energy and dynamism to a room, creating a focal point that draws attention and adds a tactile element to the experience.

  Example: A textured, layered abstract painting in a contemporary office creates an atmosphere of creative energy, inspiring out-of-the-box thinking and problem-solving.

- **Soft, Smooth Textures**: In contrast, smooth, soft textures have a calming effect, adding an element of quiet serenity to a room. These textures are well-suited to spaces where relaxation and tranquility are desired.

  Example: A smooth, flowing abstract piece in a

bedroom or spa-like bathroom creates a peaceful atmosphere, inviting viewers to unwind and relax.

Bold, rough textures evoke intensity and movement.

Choosing Art That Resonates: The Journey Within

Selecting abstract art is more than just choosing something
that looks aesthetically pleasing—it's about finding pieces that
resonate with you on a personal and emotional level. It requires
introspection and a willingness to explore your own emotions,
desires, and aspirations.

Ask yourself: What emotions do I want to evoke in this

space? What kind of energy do I want to cultivate? By answering these questions and trusting your instincts, you'll find that the right pieces of art will naturally emerge, connecting with your unique emotional landscape.

Shaping Your Emotional Landscape: Art as a Companion

Your abstract art collection is not just decoration—it becomes an integral part of your emotional and physical space. These artworks have the potential to inspire, console, motivate, and soothe, influencing your daily experiences and overall well-being.

As you continue to curate your collection, you'll find that abstract art has the power to shape not only the physical dimensions of your space but also the emotional and psychological dimensions of your life.

The Transformative Power of Abstract Art

We've only scratched the surface of the profound relationship between abstract art, emotions, and the spaces we inhabit. Abstract art has the capacity to transform your environment, stimulating creativity, promoting relaxation, and creating an inspiring atmosphere that reflects your unique emotional tapestry.

2

∿

Positive Energy

In the world of interior design, where aesthetics intertwine with the delicate balance of energy, the ancient practice of Feng Shui serves as an enduring guide. Feng Shui principles focus on the harmonious flow of energy (or qi) within a space, using colors, shapes, and arrangement to enhance well-being. In this chapter, we'll explore how the synergy between abstract art and Feng Shui can create environments where positive energy flows effortlessly, nurturing not only visual beauty but also emotional and spiritual harmony.

Abstract Art and Feng Shui Principles

Feng Shui, which translates to "wind-water" in English, is an ancient Chinese practice concerned with arranging spaces to promote harmony, balance, and auspicious energy flow. Its core idea is to channel natural forces for the benefit of the occupants' well-being, prosperity, and health. With its focus on colors, forms, and the strategic arrangement of objects, Feng Shui aligns perfectly with the transformative potential of abstract art. By thoughtfully choosing and placing abstract art, we can elevate both the energy and aesthetics of any space.

The Energetic Palette: Colors That Speak Volumes

In Feng Shui, color acts as a vibrant conduit for energy, each hue carrying its own psychological weight and energetic impact. The use of color in abstract art offers a unique way to channel and direct energy in your home or office. Let's dive deeper into the energetic meanings behind key colors in Feng Shui and explore how abstract art can amplify those energies.

- **Red: A Bold Call to Action**
  Bold and passionate, red is a color that signifies energy, vitality, and courage. Its transformative power can ignite enthusiasm, foster passion, and stimulate creativity.

  Example: Imagine a vibrant red abstract art piece hanging in the southern or southwestern corners of your office. This dynamic artwork serves as a catalyst for creativity, inspiring bold ideas and igniting enthusiasm in your workspace.
- **Blue: The Serenity of Still Waters**
  Blue symbolizes calm, serenity, and introspection. Its soothing qualities invite peace and tranquility, making it ideal for spaces dedicated to reflection, meditation, or relaxation.

  Example: In your meditation room, a soothing blue

abstract artwork placed in the northern or eastern regions enhances the tranquil atmosphere. The soft hues of blue help deepen your meditation practice and foster inner calm.

- **Green: A Symbol of Balance and Growth**
As a color associated with harmony, renewal, and growth, green fosters a sense of equilibrium and fresh energy. It's the perfect choice for spaces where personal development and balance are desired.

    Example: A green abstract art piece placed in the eastern or southeastern corners of your living room nurtures growth, renewal, and emotional balance. This art subtly promotes your personal aspirations, encouraging progress and harmony within your home.

The Choreography of Energy: Patterns That Inspire

Abstract art, with its dynamic and often intricate patterns, mirrors the principles of Feng Shui, which emphasizes the flow of energy within a space. Through the deliberate use of shapes and patterns, abstract art becomes a tool for influencing the movement and quality of energy (qi).

- **Geometric Patterns: Precision and Focus**
Geometric abstract art, characterized by sharp lines and structured shapes, resonates with the principles of order and clarity in Feng Shui. These patterns evoke focus, discipline, and mental sharpness, making them ideal for workspaces or areas requiring concentration.

    Example: In an office, abstract art featuring geometric

patterns strategically placed in the western or north-western regions enhances productivity. The precision of these patterns fosters an environment conducive to focused work and creativity.

- **Organic Patterns: Flow and Comfort**

In contrast, flowing organic shapes in abstract art evoke a sense of ease, comfort, and connection. These forms, reminiscent of the natural world, promote relaxation and emotional well-being, making them perfect for social and communal spaces.

Example: In your living room, organic abstract patterns placed in the central or northeastern regions encourage relaxation and connection. These pieces create a fluid and inviting atmosphere, making the space ideal for fostering deep conversations and peaceful interactions.

Geometric abstract art evokes focus, discipline, and
mental sharpness, making it ideal for workspaces or areas
requiring concentration.

The Art of Positioning: Placing with Purpose

Feng Shui places significant emphasis on the strategic position-
ing of elements to ensure optimal energy flow. The way you
position your abstract art has a profound impact on both the
visual harmony of the room and the energy it generates.

- **Eye-Level Connection**
  When hanging abstract art, ensure it's positioned at eye

level, creating an immediate and powerful connection between the viewer and the artwork. This placement invites engagement and allows the piece to fully influence the energy of the space.

Example: In your dining area, a vibrant abstract art piece placed at eye level creates a visual focal point, encouraging meaningful conversations and deepening connections during meals. It transforms ordinary dining into memorable, enriching experiences.

- **Simplicity and Space**

The principle of simplicity is key in Feng Shui. Avoid overcrowding your space with too many art pieces, as clutter disrupts the flow of energy and creates a sense of chaos.

Example: In a minimalist living room, allow each abstract artwork to have ample breathing space, highlighting its individual energy and visual impact. By doing so, you create a serene, harmonious environment where each piece can shine.

- **Balancing the Space**

Balance is central to Feng Shui. When placing abstract art, consider the visual and energetic balance of the space. Each piece should complement the overall energy flow rather than overpowering it.

Example: In your bedroom, opt for calming, balanced abstract art that promotes tranquility and restful energy. Place the artwork symmetrically to ensure a sense of equilibrium, which enhances relaxation and rejuvenation.

The Flow of Energy: Unlocking Abstract Art's Full Potential

By aligning abstract art with Feng Shui principles, you can unlock the full potential of both the art and the space it inhabits. Colors, shapes, and placements work together to cultivate an environment where positive energy flows freely, promoting balance, well-being, and a sense of harmony.

When selected and positioned with intention, abstract art can elevate your emotional, mental, and spiritual well-being. It becomes more than a visual element—it becomes an expression of the energy you wish to cultivate within your space. Abstract art, in this sense, is a dynamic tool for transforming not only the physical aesthetics of your surroundings but also the energetic flow and emotional atmosphere that shape your daily life.

Crafting Environments of Positive Energy

The synergy between abstract art and Feng Shui principles offers limitless possibilities for enhancing your living and working spaces. By thoughtfully integrating color, pattern, and placement, you can craft environments where positive energy abounds, nurturing your emotional and spiritual well-being. The art becomes a reflection of the energy you wish to manifest, creating a profound sense of harmony and balance that permeates every aspect of your life.

3

Nurturing the Soul

In the hustle and bustle of modern life, finding moments of serenity and inner peace is a precious gift. Abstract art, with its boundless capacity to evoke emotions and stir the soul, offers a sanctuary for those seeking solace and tranquility. Whether through mindful contemplation or active creation, abstract art serves as a powerful tool for relaxation, meditation, and emotional healing. In this chapter, we'll delve into the profound connection between abstract art and wellbeing, exploring how it can become an integral part of nurturing the soul.

The Therapeutic Canvas: A Gateway to Emotional Healing

Abstract art, with its open-ended forms and absence of concrete representations, allows viewers to engage with their imagination. This quality makes abstract art an ideal medium for therapeutic purposes, inviting individuals to project their emotions and thoughts onto the canvas. It provides a visual landscape where emotions can be explored, expressed, and understood.

A Journey Within: Meditation Through Abstract Art

Abstract art can serve as a visual gateway to meditation, offering a focal point for the mind to rest upon. By gazing at abstract pieces, you can enter a meditative state, allowing the art to guide you into deeper layers of introspection and relaxation.

- **Example:** You designate a serene corner in your home for meditation. In this space, you hang a captivating abstract painting. As you sit in quiet contemplation, your gaze drifts to the artwork, and you find yourself immersed in its intricate patterns and colors. The art becomes a portal, helping you transcend everyday concerns and guiding you on a journey within. Each session with the artwork deepens your connection to your inner self, nurturing a sense of peace and balance.

By engaging with abstract art in this way, it becomes more than just a visual experience—it transforms into a meditative practice that fosters mindfulness and serenity.

Emotional Resonance: Healing Through Visual Expression

Abstract art has the power to evoke and release buried emotions. When you encounter a piece that resonates with your inner feelings, it can create a sense of catharsis. This process of connecting with the artwork allows you to acknowledge and process emotions, facilitating emotional healing.

- **Example**: After experiencing a personal loss, you struggle with feelings of grief and sadness. During a visit to a gallery, you come across an abstract painting that captures the turmoil of your emotions through its chaotic brushstrokes and dark hues. As you spend time with the artwork, you feel a sense of release. The painting mirrors your inner world, allowing you to confront your emotions in a safe space. This connection with the art becomes the first step toward emotional healing.

Abstract art's open interpretation allows it to become a mirror of your emotional landscape, offering solace and a pathway to emotional well-being.

Mindful Contemplation: Stress Reduction Through Art

In a world filled with constant distractions, abstract art offers an opportunity for mindful contemplation. Observing abstract art mindfully encourages you to stay present in the moment, shifting your focus away from stress and worries. The colors, forms, and textures on the canvas become a source of serenity, helping you unwind and release tension.

- **Example**: After a long, stressful day, you retreat to your living room, where a soothing abstract painting adorns the wall. You sit in a comfortable chair and allow your gaze to rest on the artwork. As you immerse yourself in the calming colors and fluid forms, you feel the tension in your body gradually melt away. The art becomes a refuge, allowing you to reconnect with a sense of calm and tranquility.

Mindful observation of abstract art can serve as a powerful stress-reduction technique, offering a quiet moment of peace amidst the chaos of daily life.

Creating Your Sanctuary: Designing Spaces for Wellbeing

Abstract art can be an essential component of spaces dedicated to healing and relaxation. Whether in a meditation room, yoga studio, or a relaxation nook, abstract art can serve as a visual anchor, enhancing the atmosphere and promoting a sense of wellbeing.

- **Example**: You decide to create a personal sanctuary in your home, where you can retreat for quiet reflection and meditation. You carefully select abstract art pieces that evoke feelings of peace and serenity. Each artwork is chosen for its ability to transport you to a place of inner calm. When you enter your sanctuary, the art envelops you in an atmosphere of stillness, making it easier to relax and rejuvenate.

Incorporating abstract art into these spaces transforms them into sacred environments where wellbeing and self-care are nurtured.

Healing Through Creation: Expressing Emotions on the Canvas

For many, engaging in the creation of abstract art can be a therapeutic process in itself. Painting, drawing, or sculpting allows individuals to externalize their emotions, channeling them onto the canvas in a process that is both creative and cathartic. The act of creating becomes a journey of self-expression and healing.

- **Example**: You're going through a challenging period in your life and decide to take up abstract painting as a form of self-therapy. You pour your emotions onto the canvas, using bold colors and dynamic brushstrokes to express the inner turmoil you've been feeling. As you work, you experience a sense of release and clarity. The process of painting allows you to make sense of your emotions, and by the time you finish, you feel lighter and more at peace.

Engaging in abstract art creation allows you to process

complex emotions and express yourself in ways that words cannot capture, offering a unique form of emotional healing.

A Path to Self-Discovery: Reflecting on Art and the Self

Abstract art often prompts introspection. When you engage with these pieces, you may find yourself reflecting not only on the artwork but on your own perceptions, thoughts, and feelings. This reflection can become a powerful tool for self-discovery and personal growth.

- **Example**: During a visit to an art museum, you encounter an abstract sculpture that leaves you intrigued and contemplative. As you stand before it, you begin to question its meaning, only to realize that your interpretations reveal much about your own experiences and perspectives. This moment of reflection sparks a deeper understanding of your own thought processes, leading to new insights about yourself.

Abstract art offers an opportunity for introspection, encouraging you to explore the relationship between the art and your inner self.

Abstract art offers an opportunity for introspection.

Wellbeing in Every Brushstroke: Exploring Art as a Hobby

Engaging with abstract art need not be a passive experience. For those who enjoy hands-on creativity, experimenting with abstract art techniques can be a fulfilling and rejuvenating pursuit. Whether through painting, drawing, or sculpting, the process of creating abstract art can bring a sense of accomplishment and joy.

- **Example:** You decide to explore abstract painting as a

hobby. Armed with a blank canvas and an array of acrylic paints, you let your intuition guide your brushstrokes, allowing the colors and shapes to flow naturally. With each painting, you discover a new facet of your creativity, and the process itself becomes a source of relaxation and fulfillment.

The act of creating art adds to your overall wellbeing, providing an outlet for self-expression and a space for personal discovery.

Nurturing the Soul: Embracing the Beauty of Abstraction

Abstract art invites you to embrace the beauty of ambiguity and the power of imagination. It encourages you to let go of the need for concrete answers or clear representations, allowing your mind to wander freely. This openness can nurture the soul, offering moments of inner peace and reflection.

- **Example:** You attend an abstract art exhibition featuring a wide range of artworks, each more intriguing than the last. As you move from one piece to another, you let go of the need to fully understand each one, instead allowing yourself to experience the emotions they evoke. You leave the exhibition feeling lighter, with a renewed sense of connection to your inner world.

By embracing the abstract, you open yourself to new possibilities for emotional and spiritual wellbeing.

Artistic Wellbeing: A Holistic Approach to Healing

Art and wellbeing are intricately connected. Whether you find peace in contemplation, healing through expression, or a moment of respite in creation, abstract art can be your faithful companion on the path to emotional and spiritual wellness.

- **Example**: You integrate abstract art into your daily routine, setting aside time each day to sit with a favorite piece of artwork. This practice becomes an essential part of your self-care routine, offering moments of tranquility and inspiration that support your overall wellbeing.

By cultivating a relationship with abstract art, you create a holistic approach to emotional and spiritual health.

Nourishing the Soul: A Journey of Emotional Renewal

In the world of abstract art, you have the opportunity to nourish your soul, heal your heart, and explore the intricate landscapes of your own consciousness. It's a journey of self-discovery and emotional renewal—one that offers the gift of peace, healing, and connection.

- **Example**: You share your love for abstract art with a close friend who is going through a difficult time. Together, you explore the world of abstract expression, using it as a means of coping and healing. Your shared artistic journey becomes a source of strength and connection, enriching both of your lives.

Abstract art is not just a visual experience; it's a pathway to wellbeing that invites you to connect with yourself and others on a deeper, more meaningful level.

4

Conversation Starters

Abstract art is far more than a visual experience; it serves as a powerful gateway to conversation, connection, and shared discovery. Its ability to evoke emotions and provoke thought makes it an ideal catalyst for engaging dialogue, breaking the ice, and forging memorable connections. In this chapter, we'll explore how abstract art can become a tool for starting conversations in your living and working spaces. By strategically placing art with unique stories or personal significance, you can create environments that encourage dialogue, spark curiosity, and leave a lasting impression on your guests.

The Art of Conversation: Abstract as a Catalyst

Imagine hosting a gathering at your home. Your guests have just arrived, the atmosphere is warm, and everyone is eager to mingle—but how do you spark those conversations that lead to deeper connections? How do you ensure that guests feel comfortable and engaged? The answer often lies in the art that surrounds you.

Abstract art, with its open-ended interpretations and visually stimulating forms, provides a natural entry point for conversation. Unlike representational art, which often provides viewers with a clear narrative, abstract art invites individuals to explore their own feelings, thoughts, and interpretations. This creates a dynamic and interactive experience, allowing each viewer to contribute to the conversation with their unique perspective.

Art with Unique Stories: A Window into Your World

Every piece of abstract art has its own story, whether it's the artist's creative journey, the circumstances under which you acquired the piece, or the personal meaning it holds for you. Sharing these stories with your guests transforms the artwork into a living narrative, inviting others into a deeper dialogue.

- **Example**: Imagine an abstract painting in your living room that you discovered during a memorable trip to a remote art gallery. As your guests admire the piece, you share the story of how you stumbled upon the gallery, your interaction with the artist, and what drew you to the painting. This personal tale not only brings the artwork to life but also serves as a captivating conversation starter, encouraging guests to share their own travel experiences or artistic discoveries.

The stories behind your art make your home more than just a collection of objects—it becomes a space rich with meaning, where each piece has a voice that can spark new connections.

The story of how an artwork was acquired brings it to life.

Personal Significance: Reflecting Your Life Journey

Abstract art can also hold deep personal significance, serving as a reflection of your unique tastes, experiences, and milestones. When strategically placed, these artworks become mirrors of your personality and values, inviting guests to learn more about your life journey.

- **Example**: In your home office, you might display an abstract artwork that you commissioned to commemorate a major life event, such as a milestone birthday, a career achievement, or a personal transformation. When guests inquire about the artwork, you can share the emotional significance behind it—whether it represents a turning point in your life or a period of growth. This opens the door to meaningful conversations about your experiences and invites others to share their own stories of personal transformation.

By choosing abstract art that reflects your personal journey, you create spaces that not only showcase your taste but also foster deeper, more intimate conversations with those who enter your home.

Creating Memorable Spaces: Strategic Placement for Impact

The placement of abstract art is key to its effectiveness as a conversation starter. Where you choose to display each piece can dramatically influence the flow of dialogue and set the tone for interactions.

- **Entryway**: The entryway is the first impression your guests have of your home, making it an ideal location for a visually striking piece of abstract art. A bold artwork here immediately grabs attention and invites guests to engage from the moment they walk in.

    Example: Imagine a vibrant, large-scale abstract piece in your entryway. As guests arrive, their eyes are drawn to its bold colors and dynamic shapes. You seize the opportunity to share the backstory of the piece, whether it's the artist's intention, your own interpretation, or how the artwork aligns with your home's energy. This creates an instant icebreaker, welcoming guests into your world of creativity and personal expression.

- **Dining Room**: The dining room is a natural gathering place for friends and family, where conversation and connection flourish. Displaying thought-provoking art in this space can enhance the dining experience, encouraging guests to reflect on the artwork and engage in discussions that extend beyond the meal.

    Example: Picture an abstract artwork in your dining room that represents a specific artistic movement or cultural influence. As you enjoy dinner with your guests, they might comment on the artwork's bold forms or vibrant colors, prompting a conversation about the piece's significance. This leads to deeper discussions about art history, cultural heritage, or personal interpretations, turning an ordinary meal into a rich, meaningful experience.

- **Home Office**: Abstract art in a home office isn't just a decorative element; it can serve as a conversation starter with clients or colleagues, humanizing the professional environment and fostering a more personal connection.

    Example: If you meet clients in your home office,

consider placing abstract art with a unique backstory. As you discuss business matters, the artwork can provide a refreshing break in the conversation, allowing you to share its story and create a more relaxed, personal connection with your clients. This helps establish rapport and opens the door for further dialogue.

- **Living Room**: The living room is often the social hub of the home, where guests gather for both casual and formal interactions. It's the perfect place to display art with personal significance, giving your visitors insight into your passions and interests.

    Example: Displaying an abstract piece that reflects your love for nature, technology, or a specific art form gives your guests an opportunity to connect with you on a deeper level. Whether it's a discussion about shared hobbies or an exploration of how the artwork resonates with their own experiences, the piece acts as a bridge that fosters meaningful connections.

Enhancing Gatherings and Experiences

Incorporating abstract art as conversation starters not only enhances the visual appeal of your space but also enriches the quality of gatherings and experiences. Art becomes a bridge between individuals, encouraging meaningful exchanges, shared reflections, and memorable interactions.

Example: Consider hosting an art-themed gathering in your home, where friends and acquaintances are invited to appreciate your collection of abstract art. As the evening unfolds, you can share the stories and inspirations behind each piece, and encourage your guests to express their thoughts and interpretations. This interactive experience leads to profound conversations about creativity, personal expression, and the role of art in our lives, leaving a lasting impression on everyone involved.

The Social Power of Abstract Art

As you explore the potential of abstract art as a conversation starter, you'll find that your spaces become not only visually captivating but also socially enriching. By selecting art with personal meaning or unique stories, and placing it in strategic locations, you transform your home or office into a space where meaningful connections are sparked. The stories, emotions, and conversations that art brings into your life will leave a lasting impression on both you and your guests, making every interaction a memorable and meaningful one.

5

Personalized Art

In the vast world of interior design and art appreciation, the possibilities for enhancing your living and working spaces are seemingly endless. From modern art galleries to online art retailers, there is no shortage of options to adorn your walls. But what if you're looking for something truly one-of-a-kind, something that not only reflects your personality but also harmonizes perfectly with the ambiance of your space?

The answer lies in **personalized art**—art that is custom-made for you, tailored to your vision, and designed to complement your surroundings in a way that mass-produced pieces cannot. In this chapter, we will explore the world of custom abstract art and how commissioning bespoke pieces can transform your environment into a true reflection of your individuality.

The Power of Personalization

Your home or workspace is a reflection of who you are—your tastes, experiences, and aspirations. It should tell a story that is uniquely yours. While many ready-made art pieces are beautiful and impactful, they might not capture the essence of your personality or fit seamlessly into the specific character of your space. This is where personalized art comes into play, allowing you to collaborate with an artist to create a masterpiece that resonates with your vision and enhances the energy of your environment.

Personalized art is not just a decorative element; it's a meaningful extension of who you are. It speaks to your passions, interests, and experiences in a way that is deeply personal and often emotionally resonant. By investing in custom abstract art, you have the opportunity to elevate your space with pieces that are not only visually stunning but also imbued with significance.

The Art of Commissioning Custom Abstract Art

Commissioning a piece of custom abstract art is a rewarding, collaborative process that allows you to bring your vision to life with the help of a skilled artist. The journey from concept to creation is an intimate experience, resulting in an artwork that feels like an extension of your personality and the atmosphere you want to cultivate.

1. **Initial Consultation**: The process begins with a conversation. During this consultation, you'll share your ideas,

preferences, and the mood or emotions you want the artwork to evoke. This is your opportunity to provide the artist with a deep understanding of what you envision for your space.

- ○ **Example**: Imagine you're redecorating your beachfront condo. In your initial consultation, you describe to the artist your love for the sea, your desire for a peaceful yet energizing atmosphere, and your preference for cool blue tones. You also mention your passion for sailing. These insights form the foundation for your custom abstract piece, as the artist listens carefully to your vision and translates it into a conceptual design.

2. **Concept Development**: Once the artist has a clear understanding of your vision, they will begin developing sketches and ideas for your artwork. This stage is highly collaborative, allowing you to provide feedback and fine-tune the concept until it aligns perfectly with your expectations.

- ○ **Example**: The artist presents you with several sketches, each incorporating elements that capture the essence of the sea and sailing. One sketch stands out—a composition that balances the serenity of the ocean with the dynamic energy of the waves. You work together with the artist to refine the design, deciding to include subtle nautical elements, such as hints of silver leaf to mimic the reflection of moonlight on water.

3. **Creation of the Artwork**: With the concept finalized, the artist moves into the creation phase. During this stage, they carefully select colors, textures, and techniques that bring your vision to life. Depending on your preferences, you might be involved in providing feedback throughout the creation process.

   ○ **Example**: As the artist works on your custom piece, layers of paint and texture come together to evoke the sensation of waves crashing against the shore. The finished artwork features sweeping brushstrokes in cool blues and greens, while delicate silver accents capture the shimmer of the ocean at dusk. When you see the final product, you're awed by how perfectly it encapsulates the tranquility and adventure you hoped to convey.

4. **Presentation and Placement**: Once the artwork is complete, the artist presents the piece to you and helps determine the best location for it within your space. The presentation is often an emotional moment, as the artwork is revealed in all its beauty.

   ○ **Example**: You and the artist meet at your beachfront condo for the grand reveal. As the artwork is unveiled, you're overcome with emotion—it's even more breathtaking than you imagined. After discussing placement options, you decide to display the piece in your living room, where it becomes the focal point of the space, admired by both you and your guests.

Tailoring Art to Your Space's Ambiance

One of the most remarkable aspects of personalized art is its ability to harmonize with the unique ambiance of your space. Whether your goal is to create a serene retreat, a dynamic and productive workspace, or a cozy and inviting environment for family and friends, custom abstract art can be tailored to align perfectly with the mood you want to set.

- **Example**: If your home office is designed to be a hub of creativity and productivity, you might commission an abstract piece that features vibrant colors and bold geometric shapes. This energizing artwork complements the dynamic atmosphere, helping to fuel your work ethic and spark new ideas.

- **Example**: In contrast, if you're looking to enhance a cozy reading nook, you could collaborate with an artist to create a custom piece inspired by your favorite literary quotes. Each brushstroke in this personalized artwork resonates with your love for literature, turning the space into a sanctuary for reflection and imagination.

You might commission an abstract painting featuring
your favorite literary quote.

Beyond Personal Preference: Art as a Conversation Starter

While personalized art beautifully reflects your individuality, it also serves as a captivating conversation starter. Guests and visitors will be naturally drawn to the unique piece, intrigued by its story and the collaborative process that brought it to life.

- **Example**: During a dinner party at your home, friends and family are captivated by the custom abstract artwork in your living room. Its vibrant colors and intricate details spark curiosity, leading to a conversation about the piece's origin. You share the story of how you commissioned the artwork, describing the artist's process and the personal significance behind each element. As you discuss the journey of creation, your guests feel more connected to both you and the artwork, and the conversation flows effortlessly.

This blend of personal meaning and artistic collaboration turns your home into a place where not only art is appreciated, but also stories are shared, and deeper connections are made.

The Timeless Value of Custom Art

Unlike mass-produced art that can be found in countless homes and offices, custom abstract art holds a timeless value that is deeply personal. It's not just an object of decoration; it's a reflection of your journey, your experiences, and your artistic vision. As time passes, this unique piece becomes a cherished part of your life—perhaps even an heirloom that can be passed down to future generations.

- **Example**: Decades from now, the custom artwork you commissioned still graces the walls of your beachfront condo. It serves as a testament to your love for the sea, your passion for adventure, and your appreciation for art. As it's passed down through your family, the piece continues to tell the story of your life, connecting generations with shared memories and a legacy of artistic expression.

Embark on a Personalized Artistic Journey

The world of personalized abstract art invites you to embark on a creative journey that is uniquely your own. By commissioning custom pieces, you not only enhance the beauty and atmosphere of your living or working spaces, but you also infuse them with the essence of your personality and aspirations. Your surroundings become more than just a physical space—they become a canvas for your story, a testament to your individuality, and a source of inspiration for everyone who enters.

- **Example**: As you sit in your living room, gazing upon the custom artwork that adorns the wall, you are reminded of the initial consultation, the artist's sketches, and the creative process that brought your vision to life. This artwork is a masterpiece that reflects your soul, a source of pride that elevates your space to new heights of aesthetic and emotional fulfillment.

So why settle for mass-produced art when you can create something truly exceptional? Join the ranks of those who have discovered the transformative power of personalized art, and bring your vision to life, one brushstroke at a time.

6

Personalizing Shared Spaces

Shared spaces, whether in homes or offices, can sometimes feel impersonal or lack cohesion. Abstract art has the unique ability to transform these spaces into personalized environments that reflect the values, tastes, and identities of those who use them. In this chapter, we will explore how abstract art can be used to inject individuality and creativity into shared spaces, fostering connection and enhancing the ambiance of the environment.

The Power of Abstract Art in Shared Spaces

Shared spaces, by their nature, are used by multiple people with different tastes, preferences, and purposes. Whether it's a communal living area in a home or a meeting space in an office, these environments require careful thought to ensure that they are welcoming, functional, and reflective of the collective identity of those who use them. Abstract art, with its ability to be open to interpretation, provides the perfect canvas for creating spaces that feel personal yet adaptable to everyone's needs.

- **Example**: In a shared family living room, an abstract painting featuring soothing earth tones and organic shapes can provide a calming backdrop while still allowing each family member to find their own personal connection to the piece. Some may see nature in the shapes, while others may interpret the flow of colors as symbolic of their family's dynamic energy.

Choosing Abstract Art for Shared Spaces

When selecting abstract art for shared spaces, it's important to choose pieces that resonate with the shared values or purpose of the space. Here are some key considerations:

1. **Neutral Yet Impactful**
   Neutral colors and abstract forms can make a space feel cohesive without overpowering the personal identities of those who use the area. Opt for pieces that balance simplicity with intrigue.

   - **Example**: A large canvas featuring soft grays, beiges, and whites can unify the decor of a shared living room, while the texture and shapes of the painting add interest and dimension, encouraging subtle yet engaging conversations.

2. **Reflecting a Common Identity**

In offices or other collaborative environments, abstract art can help reinforce a sense of shared identity. Choose art that embodies the company's values, culture, or mission.

- **Example**: A modern tech company might select bold abstract pieces that emphasize innovation and forward-thinking, featuring geometric shapes or vibrant colors that represent progress and creativity.

1. **Open to Interpretation**

One of the strengths of abstract art is its ambiguity. Each viewer can interpret the piece differently, which makes it an ideal fit for shared spaces where people might have varying tastes and viewpoints.

- **Example**: A colorful, playful abstract mural in a shared office break room can inspire a wide range of reactions—from creativity to relaxation—allowing each employee to connect with the piece in their own way.

Each employee connects with a piece in their own way.

Creating Zones of Expression

Another powerful way to personalize shared spaces with abstract art is by using it to define specific zones within an area. Abstract art can create a visual separation between different functions in a room, giving each zone its own identity while maintaining cohesion.

- **Example**: In an open-concept office, abstract art can help define different spaces for collaboration, individual work, and relaxation. A bright, abstract piece with dynamic lines can energize a brainstorming zone, while a more subdued, calming piece might anchor a quiet reading or meditation nook.

Encouraging Collaboration Through Art

Incorporating abstract art into shared spaces can also foster collaboration and connection. Interactive abstract pieces that allow people to engage with the art can stimulate conversation, encourage teamwork, and enhance the creative process.

- **Example**: In a co-working space, an interactive abstract sculpture that changes shape or color depending on how it's touched can become a playful focal point, encouraging spontaneous conversation and collaboration among users.

Final Thoughts: Personalizing the Shared Experience

By introducing abstract art into shared spaces, you invite individuality and creativity into environments that might otherwise feel impersonal or generic. The flexibility and interpretive nature of abstract art make it the perfect tool for enhancing these spaces, giving them warmth, personality, and a sense of ownership for everyone involved.

7

Thematic Rooms

Imagine walking into a room where every detail, from the furniture to the smallest decor element, revolves around a unifying theme—an abstract art piece that serves as both the anchor and the creative catalyst for the space. Thematic rooms offer a unique opportunity to create a cohesive and immersive environment, where art isn't just decoration but the heartbeat of the entire design.

In this chapter, we'll explore how you can use abstract art as the driving force behind your interior design, crafting rooms that are both visually captivating and deeply personal.

The Power of a Unifying Theme

Thematic rooms are more than just well-coordinated spaces; they are a reflection of how art and design can converge to tell a story. A central theme, inspired by an abstract art piece, allows for the seamless integration of colors, shapes, textures, and emotions, resulting in a room that feels harmonious and intentional. By placing abstract art at the center of your design process, you can transform a room into a living canvas where every element contributes to the overall ambiance.

Choosing Your Muse: Selecting the Perfect Abstract Art Piece

The first step in creating a thematic room is selecting an abstract art piece that resonates with you. This artwork will act as your muse, inspiring the color palette, mood, and over-all aesthetic of the room. Whether it's a painting, sculpture, or mixed-media installation, the art you choose should evoke emotions and speak to your personal style.

- **Example:** You've discovered an abstract painting that embodies the essence of movement and freedom. The vibrant blues and greens, combined with bold brush-strokes, give the impression of wind and waves. The energy of the piece inspires you to create a room centered around the concept of fluidity and flow. This artwork will serve as the heart of your thematic room.

When selecting your muse, look for abstract art that not only complements the space but also ignites your creativity. It should be a piece that you feel deeply connected to—one that will influence the mood and design of the entire room.

Defining Your Theme: Let the Art Guide You

Once you've chosen your abstract art piece, the next step is to define the theme of the room. The artwork will naturally offer clues about its core elements—whether it's the colors, shapes, or emotions it evokes. Let these elements guide your exploration of the theme.

- **Example**: Your abstract painting, with its swirling blues and greens, evokes the feeling of waves and wind in motion. The overall mood is one of freedom and fluidity, inspiring you to create a room that embodies these elements. You decide to define the theme as "Fluid Freedom," focusing on movement, natural elements, and a sense of openness.

By allowing the abstract art to inform the theme, you create a cohesive design that feels organic and true to the essence of the artwork. The theme should be broad enough to allow for creativity but specific enough to give the room a sense of purpose and identity.

Creating a Cohesive Design: Furniture and Decor That Align with the Theme

With your theme established, it's time to choose furniture and decor that align with the artistic vision. Each piece should complement the abstract art, either by mirroring its colors, shapes, or textures. Think of the room as a curated space, where every item works together to enhance the overall ambiance.

- **Example**: For your "Fluid Freedom" room, you select a deep blue sofa with soft, wave-like patterns that echo the movement in your abstract painting. The coffee table features a glass top that reflects the colors of the sea, while throw pillows in shades of teal and green add a touch of freshness. Sculptures and vases with flowing, organic shapes complete the decor, creating a space that feels alive and in motion.

The goal is to create a design that feels cohesive without being overly matchy. Each piece should feel like a natural extension of the theme, contributing to the overall harmony of the room.

Lighting and Ambiance: Setting the Mood

Lighting plays a crucial role in creating the right atmosphere for your thematic room. The right lighting can enhance the abstract art, highlighting its details and creating mood-enhancing shadows that align with the theme. Choose fixtures that complement the room's design and art piece.

- **Example**: In your "Fluid Freedom" room, you choose a pendant light with a cascading design that mimics the fluid movement of water. The soft, diffused lighting creates a tranquil and inviting atmosphere, allowing the bold colors of the abstract painting to take center stage. Additionally, strategically placed accent lighting helps to highlight key decor elements, adding depth and dimension to the room.

By carefully selecting the lighting, you can transform the room into an immersive experience where every detail, from the shadows to the highlights, enhances the thematic ambiance.

Personalization and Details: Infusing Your Personality

While the abstract art serves as the muse for your thematic room, it's important to infuse the space with elements of your own personality. Personal touches, such as custom-made decor, meaningful items, or family heirlooms, can help make the room feel like an authentic expression of who you are.

- **Example**: To add a personal touch to your "Fluid Freedom" room, you create a custom coffee table that features a glass top filled with a collage of your favorite beach photographs. This personalized element reinforces the theme of movement and freedom while also making the room feel more intimate and reflective of your experiences.

Personalizing your thematic room allows you to create a space that feels truly yours—a place where art and life intersect in meaningful ways.

A personalized, thematic room reflects may reflect your experiences.

Achieving Visual Harmony: Layout and Arrangement

The layout of the room plays a significant role in how the abstract art is experienced. The arrangement of furniture and decor should draw attention to the central art piece, ensuring that it remains the focal point of the space.

- **Example**: In your "Fluid Freedom" room, the abstract painting takes pride of place above the sofa. The furniture is arranged in a way that naturally directs the eye toward the artwork, allowing it to be the first thing any-one notices when entering the room. The layout is open and fluid, mirroring the theme of the art, and creating a sense of movement and flow throughout the space.

By carefully arranging the furniture and decor, you ensure that the room feels balanced and harmonious, with the abstract art acting as the central thread that ties everything together.

The Art of Transformation: Embracing Change

Thematic rooms are not static; they are dynamic spaces that can evolve over time. Don't be afraid to update or rearrange elements to keep the room feeling fresh and inspiring. As seasons change, so can your decor, allowing the room to adapt to different moods and occasions.

- **Example**: As summer turns to fall, you introduce new textiles and decor to your "Fluid Freedom" room. Bright throw blankets and beach-themed accessories are swapped out for cozy, warm-toned accents, creating a different ambiance while still staying true to the room's overall theme. This flexibility keeps the space engaging and ensures it continues to reflect your evolving tastes.

Allowing your thematic room to evolve keeps it alive and relevant, while still maintaining the core elements that define the space.

Abstract Art as the Heartbeat of Design

When you allow abstract art to guide your design process, you're not just creating a well-coordinated room—you're crafting an experience. Thematic rooms centered around abstract art offer a way to explore the synergy between creativity, design, and personal expression. The art becomes the heartbeat of the room, shaping its mood and influencing every design choice.

- **Example**: Friends and family who enter your "Fluid Freedom" room often remark on its serene and welcoming atmosphere. They are drawn to the abstract painting that graces the wall, and conversations naturally revolve around its beauty and the emotions it evokes. The room becomes a testament to the power of thematic design, where every detail contributes to a harmonious and immersive experience.

By creating thematic rooms, you not only transform your living spaces but also invite others into a world where art and design coexist in perfect harmony.

8

⌘

Aesthetics and Functionality

In the ever-evolving world of interior design, the concept of space has become increasingly dynamic. As modern living and working environments embrace open floor plans and multifunctional spaces, the need for creative and functional room dividers has never been more apparent. Traditional room dividers—while practical—often lack the visual appeal and impact that contemporary spaces demand. Enter large abstract art pieces as room dividers, a design choice that seamlessly merges aesthetics with utility. In this chapter, we explore how these captivating artworks can redefine your spaces while adding both functionality and artistic allure.

The Evolution of Room Dividers

Room dividers have a long history in interior design, from folding screens in ancient China to modern partitions used to delineate space in open-plan homes and offices. Traditionally, dividers served a purely functional role—segmenting rooms for privacy or organizing space. While effective, these dividers often lacked the ability to enhance the visual appeal of the room. As design trends shifted toward more open and versatile layouts, the need for room dividers that were both functional and beautiful became clear. This is where large abstract art steps in, transforming the utilitarian concept of room dividers into an opportunity for artistic expression.

The Visual Appeal of Abstract Art

Abstract art is known for its ability to evoke emotions and capture attention through its use of color, form, and texture. When integrated into the design of a room as a divider, abstract art not only fulfills its practical purpose but also acts as a striking focal point. These pieces have the unique ability to blend seamlessly into the environment while still standing out as bold statements.

Large abstract art pieces bring a level of sophistication and visual interest to any space, offering a perfect balance of function and aesthetics. By choosing the right piece, you can redefine the flow of your room, create designated zones, and add an artistic layer that reflects your style.

Creating Visual Partitions

One of the most exciting aspects of using abstract art as a room divider is the opportunity to create visual partitions that enhance the flow and functionality of open spaces. In modern homes and offices, open floor plans are common, offering flexibility but sometimes lacking clear boundaries between different areas. Large abstract artworks provide an elegant solution to this challenge, allowing you to define distinct areas without sacrificing the open feel of the space.

- **Open Floor Plans**: In homes and modern office spaces, open floor plans can make it difficult to create distinct zones for different activities. Large abstract art pieces can serve as beautiful and effective visual partitions, helping to delineate areas such as living and dining spaces without disrupting the overall flow.

  - **Example**: Imagine a spacious loft apartment where the living room flows directly into the dining area. To create subtle separation without using traditional dividers, a massive abstract painting stands between the two spaces. Its vibrant colors and dynamic shapes draw the eye, acting as an artistic partition that maintains the openness of the loft while providing visual cues that distinguish the different zones.

- **Home Offices**: With the rise of remote work, home offices have become essential, but many people struggle to create a dedicated workspace within a larger room. A large abstract art piece can define your home office area while adding creativity and inspiration to your daily work routine.

  - **Example**: Your home office is situated in a corner

of your living room. To visually separate your workspace from the rest of the room, a substantial abstract artwork on a rotating base serves as both a room divider and an artistic centerpiece. During work hours, you turn the artwork to face your desk, creating a sense of focus and concentration. Once the workday is over, you swivel the piece to integrate it back into the living area, effortlessly blending work and leisure.

The use of a large abstract art piece as a room divider is
the perfect marriage of functionality and artistry.

Function Meets Artistry

The use of large abstract art pieces as room dividers represents the perfect marriage of functionality and artistry. These pieces not only serve a practical purpose by segmenting space, but they also enhance the overall aesthetic of the room. Let's explore how large abstract art can fulfill dual roles as both functional dividers and artistic statements.

- **Aesthetic Enhancement**: Large abstract artworks do more than divide space—they become integral parts of the room's design, contributing to its visual interest, texture, and color scheme. They serve as captivating focal points that draw attention and stimulate conversation.

  - **Example**: In a contemporary office lobby, a towering abstract sculpture divides the reception area from the waiting lounge. Its metallic finish and intricate design capture the innovative spirit of the company, leaving a lasting impression on visitors. The artwork not only provides functional separation but also reflects the company's identity and values, enhancing the overall aesthetic of the space.

- **Sound and Light Control**: In addition to visual separation, large abstract art pieces can also help manage sound and light in a space. Depending on the materials used, these artworks can improve acoustics by absorbing sound or control natural light to create the desired ambiance.

- ◦ **Example**: Your home studio is a creative sanctuary for music production. To optimize sound quality, a large abstract artwork constructed with sound-absorbing materials serves as a room divider. This functional art piece enhances the acoustics of the studio, allowing you to produce music with precision while adding a touch of artistic flair that inspires creativity.

- **Functional Flexibility**: Some large abstract art pieces are designed with added functionality in mind. These versatile works can rotate to adjust the visual partition or even incorporate storage elements, making them both practical and beautiful.

  - ◦ **Example**: Your living room transitions into an entertainment space for movie nights. A rotating abstract artwork with integrated shelving serves as both a room divider and a storage solution, housing your collection of movies and board games. The artwork's multifunctionality adds depth and character to the space while keeping it organized.

Customization and Personalization

One of the most compelling aspects of using large abstract art as room dividers is the ability to customize and personalize these pieces to suit your style, space, and functional needs. Whether you're working with an artist to create a bespoke piece or selecting a unique work that complements your décor, the possibilities for personalization are endless.

- **Example**: In a high-end restaurant, an expansive abstract artwork composed of ceramic tiles visually separates the bar from the dining area. Crafted in collaboration with a local artist, this piece not only functions as a room divider but also reflects the restaurant's commitment to art and luxury. The custom design becomes a signature element of the restaurant's identity, contributing to both its aesthetic appeal and its unique atmosphere.

By commissioning or selecting personalized abstract art, you can create room dividers that are tailored to your exact specifications, reflecting both your personal style and the specific needs of your space.

Unlocking the Potential of Large Abstract Art

In today's design landscape, large abstract art pieces are redefining how we use space. As room dividers, they go beyond mere functionality to become captivating works of art that enhance the aesthetics and purpose of your environment.

- **Example**: In a contemporary art gallery, large abstract canvases suspended from the ceiling serve as mobile room dividers. These flexible dividers allow for the fluid reconfiguration of the exhibition space, adapting to the needs of each installation while offering visitors a dynamic and immersive experience. The movable art pieces not only serve practical purposes but also add an extra layer of creativity and interaction to the gallery's design.

Whether you're looking to create distinct zones within an open space, enhance the functionality of your home office, or add an artistic touch to your interior design, consider the transformative potential of large abstract art pieces as room dividers. These works of art offer a perfect blend of function and beauty, elevating your appreciation for both artistic expression and practical design.

9

✺

Boosting Productivity

In today's fast-paced world, productivity is often seen as the key to success. As we all strive to optimize our workspaces and streamline our workflows, we sometimes overlook the powerful role that our surroundings play in enhancing our efficiency. One often underappreciated tool in boosting productivity is abstract art. Beyond its aesthetic appeal, abstract art can transform your workspace, elevate focus, and inspire creativity in ways that are subtle but powerful. In this chapter, we'll explore the psychological foundations of productivity and how abstract art, when placed strategically in offices or workspaces, can supercharge your workday.

The Psychology of Productivity

Productivity is more than just working harder or longer; it's about creating the right conditions for focused, creative, and

63

effective work. These conditions are influenced by both our mental state and our environment. Research shows that the spaces in which we work can either enhance or diminish our ability to concentrate, problem-solve, and innovate. A workspace that promotes mental clarity, reduces stress, and sparks creativity is essential for maintaining high levels of productivity.

While many productivity tools focus on task management or time optimization, abstract art offers a unique approach by influencing your environment to create a more conducive atmosphere for getting things done.

The Role of Abstract Art

Abstract art, with its dynamic forms, vibrant colors, and intricate patterns, has the potential to shape our mental state in ways that directly impact productivity. Whether by instilling a sense of order, promoting relaxation, or igniting creative thinking, abstract art can be a game-changer for both focus and efficiency. Let's explore how.

Fostering Focus with Geometric Patterns

Geometric patterns, with their precise lines and structured compositions, naturally evoke a sense of order and clarity. In a workspace, these elements help foster a focused and organized mindset. The human brain is drawn to patterns, and the repetitive, symmetrical nature of geometric shapes can act as a visual cue to promote concentration and mental discipline.

- **Example**: Imagine an office adorned with a large

geometric abstract artwork that dominates one wall. The symmetrical patterns and clean lines create an environment that's conducive to concentration. As you work, your eyes occasionally drift to the artwork, and its structured design subtly guides your thoughts toward precision, helping you stay on track with your tasks.

Geometric abstract art can be especially effective in workspaces where organization and analytical thinking are paramount, such as offices or study areas.

Soothing Colors for Stress Reduction

Colors play a vital role in shaping our emotional and mental state, and abstract art's diverse color palettes can be used to influence how we feel in a workspace. Soft, soothing colors like blues and greens are known to reduce stress and anxiety, which in turn can enhance focus and productivity.

- **Example**: Picture a corporate boardroom featuring an abstract artwork in shades of soft blue and gentle green. During high-stakes meetings or intense discussions, the calming colors help alleviate tension, enabling participants to focus on problem-solving rather than stress. The artwork creates an atmosphere of tranquility, making it easier for everyone to remain composed and productive.

By incorporating abstract art with calming colors into your workspace, you can create a stress-reducing environment that supports focused, effective work.

Calming colors in a boardroom help alleviate tension.

Stimulating Creativity with Bold Color Variety

While some colors soothe and calm, others can ignite creativity and stimulate innovative thinking. Abstract art often combines a wide variety of colors and shapes, making it an ideal tool for sparking inspiration and out-of-the-box thinking in creative work environments.

- **Example**: In a design studio, a bold, multicolored abstract painting featuring unconventional shapes can become a wellspring of inspiration. As designers work on creative projects, the artwork's vibrant hues and fluid forms serve as a visual prompt to think beyond the ordinary, pushing boundaries and encouraging fresh ideas.

This combination of dynamic colors and abstract forms creates an atmosphere where creativity thrives, making it perfect for environments like advertising agencies, creative studios, and art spaces.

Strategic Placement for Maximum Impact

Where you place abstract art within a workspace is just as important as the art itself. Strategic placement can amplify the benefits of abstract art by enhancing specific areas of focus, collaboration, or relaxation within your office. Let's look at how different placements can maximize the impact of abstract art on productivity.

- **Office Spaces**: In areas where individual focus is critical —such as workstations or private offices—abstract art that promotes concentration and mental clarity is key.

  Example: In a home office, hang a geometric abstract painting near your desk. The precise lines and structured forms act as a visual reminder to stay focused, guiding you back to your task whenever distractions arise. This strategic placement helps create a mental association between the artwork and a productive work mindset.

- **Collaborative Areas**: For spaces where teamwork and brainstorming are common, abstract art that sparks creativity and inspires innovative thinking can elevate the quality of collaborative efforts.

Example: In a marketing agency's brainstorming room, a vibrant abstract artwork with dynamic shapes and bold colors sets the tone for creative thinking. The artwork energizes the space, encouraging team members to approach problems from new angles and collaborate with a sense of excitement.

- **Reception Areas**: First impressions matter, especially in workspaces where clients or visitors regularly enter. Abstract art in reception or waiting areas can communicate professionalism and set a positive tone for interactions.

Example: In a law firm's reception area, a large abstract artwork in soothing colors creates an atmosphere of calm and professionalism. Clients, while waiting for their meetings, feel at ease, which fosters trust and confidence in their upcoming interactions.

- **Break and Relaxation Spaces**: Even in high-performance work environments, it's important to have spaces where employees can relax and recharge. Abstract art in these areas can provide a mental break, helping employees return to work refreshed and more productive.

Example: In an employee lounge, an abstract painting with organic shapes and calming colors creates a peaceful environment. This designated retreat allows employees to unwind, recharge, and return to work with renewed focus and energy.

- **Home Office Sanctuaries**: For those who work from home, abstract art can transform a home office into a personal sanctuary of productivity and creativity.

Example: In a home-based creative studio, an abstract sculpture with dynamic shapes sits on your desk. The sculpture serves as both a visual and tactile focal point, inviting you to interact with it as a way to channel its energy into your creative process.

Elevating Productivity, One Brushstroke at a Time

Incorporating abstract art into your workspace is not just about aesthetics—it's a strategic investment in your productivity and overall well-being. Whether through the precise order of geometric forms or the calming influence of soothing colors, abstract art has the power to create a workspace that fosters focus, reduces stress, and stimulates creativity.

- **Example**: Consider conducting an informal experiment in your office. Introduce a few pieces of abstract art, then track your productivity levels over the following weeks. You may be pleasantly surprised by the positive effect these visual elements have on your concentration, creativity, and overall satisfaction with your workspace.

By thoughtfully integrating abstract art into your environment, you transform your workspace from a mere functional area into a source of inspiration and efficiency. As you experiment with different styles, colors, and placements, you'll discover how abstract art can be your silent productivity partner —one brushstroke at a time—helping you achieve your goals with both style and grace.

10

Abstract Art in Functional Spaces

When we think about where to place art in our homes or offices, we often focus on living rooms, dining areas, or bedrooms—spaces designed for relaxation or socializing. However, some of the most functional spaces, like kitchens, bathrooms, and utility rooms, are often overlooked as canvases for creativity.

These rooms serve practical purposes but can be transformed into areas of visual delight with the right abstract art. In this chapter, we'll explore how abstract art can elevate these functional spaces, infusing them with color, personality, and creative energy.

Why Art in Functional Spaces?

Functional spaces are often associated with routine tasks and utilitarian design. Adding abstract art to these areas can create an unexpected touch of beauty, offering a refreshing break from the functional nature of the room. Art in kitchens, bathrooms, and utility rooms can enhance the aesthetic appeal of these spaces while providing moments of visual inspiration in everyday activities.

- **Example**: Imagine preparing your morning coffee in a kitchen that features a large, vibrant abstract painting. The artwork adds a sense of energy and liveliness to your routine, transforming an ordinary activity into something more engaging.

Kitchens: Energizing the Heart of the Home

The kitchen is often referred to as the heart of the home, and for good reason—it's where we cook, eat, and gather with family and friends. But kitchens are also highly functional spaces, filled with appliances and practical tools. Abstract art can be the perfect addition to soften the room's utilitarian feel and create a more welcoming atmosphere.

- **Choosing the Right Artwork**: In a kitchen, consider abstract art that reflects the energy and vibrancy of the space. Bold, dynamic pieces with warm colors can complement the warmth of cooking and conversation.

Alternatively, cooler tones can bring a sense of calm to a busy kitchen.

- ○ **Example**: A large abstract painting with swirling oranges, reds, and yellows could be hung above a breakfast nook or on a prominent wall near the dining area. The vibrant colors mirror the warmth and creativity of the cooking process, adding a sense of excitement to the room.
- **Placement Considerations**: Kitchens are high-traffic areas where practicality is key, so the placement of artwork should account for moisture, heat, and food splatters. Opt for pieces framed behind glass or created from durable, easy-to-clean materials like metal or acrylic.

- ○ **Example**: In a sleek, modern kitchen with stainless steel appliances, a series of small abstract prints framed in glass can be placed on the backsplash behind the counter. The glass provides protection from cooking splatters while the art adds an unexpected pop of color.

Bathrooms: Transforming Personal Retreats

Bathrooms are spaces for personal care and relaxation, making them ideal for abstract art that evokes calm, tranquility, or even a touch of luxury. A thoughtfully placed abstract piece can elevate a simple bathroom into a spa-like retreat.

- **Creating a Serene Atmosphere**: In bathrooms, abstract

art in soothing colors—like soft blues, greens, or pastels —can create a peaceful ambiance. These colors evoke the calming qualities of water and nature, making the room feel like a tranquil escape.

- ◦ **Example**: A bathroom decorated with white tiles and modern fixtures can be softened with an abstract painting in shades of blue and teal. Positioned above the bathtub, the artwork mirrors the calm of flowing water, turning the space into a sanctuary of relaxation.

- **Waterproofing and Durability**: Given the high humidity in bathrooms, it's important to choose art that can withstand moisture. Water-resistant materials such as metal prints, ceramic tiles, or laminated canvas are ideal for these spaces.

- ◦ **Example**: A large abstract mural made of waterproof tiles can be installed in the shower area. The tile's colorful, abstract design brings life to the otherwise functional space, creating a luxurious and visually stunning focal point.

- **Unexpected Placements**: Bathrooms often have smaller, overlooked areas that are perfect for art. Think about adding abstract pieces above towel racks, near mirrors, or on narrow walls to make the most of the space.

- ◦ **Example**: A small, vibrant abstract painting placed above a towel rack or beside a mirror can make a compact bathroom feel more elegant and thoughtfully designed.

A small, vibrant abstract painting placed above a towel rack or beside a mirror can make a compact bathroom feel more elegant and thoughtfully designed.

Utility Rooms: Elevating Practical Spaces

Utility rooms and laundry areas are typically designed for function, with little thought given to aesthetics. However, these rooms are often where we spend a surprising amount of time. Incorporating abstract art into these areas can transform them from purely functional spaces into more enjoyable environments.

- **Adding Color and Personality**: Utility rooms often feature muted colors or bare walls. Adding bold abstract art can infuse energy into the space, making mundane tasks like laundry more enjoyable.

  - **Example**: A vibrant abstract print featuring bold geometric patterns can be placed above a folding table in the laundry room. The bright colors and dynamic shapes add a sense of playfulness to the otherwise utilitarian space, making the room feel less like a chore and more like a creative outlet.
- **Maximizing Wall Space**: Utility rooms are often small, so wall space is precious. Use smaller abstract art pieces or create a gallery wall to make the most of limited room.

  - **Example**: In a narrow utility room, a series of small, colorful abstract prints can be arranged in a vertical line, drawing the eye upward and making the space feel taller. The artwork breaks up the monotony of the room, adding interest and dimension.
- **Functional Art**: In utility spaces, art can serve dual purposes by being both decorative and practical. Consider abstract art that doubles as storage solutions, such as decorative wall hooks or sculptural shelving units.

  - **Example**: In a small utility room, an abstract metal

sculpture with built-in hooks can serve as a place to hang cleaning supplies or towels. This piece not only adds visual interest but also maximizes storage space, making the room more efficient.

Final Thoughts: Merging Form and Function

Incorporating abstract art into functional spaces like kitchens, bathrooms, and utility rooms is a powerful way to elevate their aesthetic appeal while maintaining their practicality. Art in these areas can make routine tasks more enjoyable, create a sense of calm, and turn overlooked spaces into design features. With thoughtful placement and careful consideration of materials, abstract art can transform even the most functional spaces into rooms that inspire creativity and joy.

So, the next time you consider where to place your abstract art, don't overlook these practical spaces. With the right approach, your kitchen, bathroom, and utility room can become as artistically inspiring as any other room in your home or office.

11

Art for Small Spaces

In the world of interior design, small spaces often pose unique challenges. Whether it's a cozy apartment, a compact home office, or a narrow hallway, finding ways to bring personality and energy into these areas without overwhelming them can be tricky. Luckily, abstract art offers the perfect solution. Abstract pieces are versatile and can make a powerful impact in even the smallest of spaces. In this chapter, we'll explore how you can strategically use abstract art to elevate compact environments, adding depth, dimension, and creativity to your home or office.

The Power of Abstract Art in Small Spaces

The key to maximizing the impact of abstract art in small spaces lies in careful selection and thoughtful placement. The goal is to make the space feel larger, more dynamic, and infused with personality. Abstract art offers endless possibilities for this transformation because it doesn't rely on literal representations—its open interpretation allows it to adapt to any environment.

- **Example**: Imagine a small home office where wall space is limited. A bright, energetic abstract painting with bold lines and shapes can instantly inject creativity and vitality into the room without taking up valuable floor space. The eye is naturally drawn to the artwork, making the room feel more expansive and engaging.

Selecting the Right Art for Compact Areas

When choosing abstract art for small spaces, scale and color are critical considerations. The size of the artwork should complement the room's proportions, while the color palette should enhance the overall ambiance of the space.

- **Scale**: In smaller rooms, avoid large, overpowering pieces that can make the space feel cramped. Instead, opt for mid-sized or smaller artworks that fit comfortably on the walls without overwhelming them. Groupings of smaller pieces, like a gallery wall, can also work well to create visual interest without overpowering the room.

  - **Example**: In a narrow hallway, a series of smaller abstract paintings or prints arranged in a vertical line can draw the eye upward, making the hallway appear taller and more visually intriguing.
- **Color**: The color palette of the art should either

complement or contrast with the room's decor. Lighter, softer hues can help make a room feel more open and airy, while bold, vibrant colors can bring energy and personality to the space.

- ○ **Example**: In a small living room with neutral furnishings, a colorful abstract artwork with bright reds, oranges, and yellows can add warmth and excitement, creating a focal point that draws attention away from the room's size.

Strategic Placement: Making the Most of Your Space

Where you place the art can have a significant impact on how the room feels. In small spaces, the goal is to create a sense of openness and flow, so consider placing the artwork in ways that elongate or enhance the dimensions of the room.

- **Vertical Focus**: To make a room feel taller, choose abstract pieces with a vertical orientation. Tall, narrow paintings or sculptures draw the eye upward, creating the illusion of height. This trick works especially well in rooms with lower ceilings or limited floor space.

  - ○ **Example**: In a small dining nook, a tall abstract painting with vertical lines can make the space feel taller and more open, providing visual interest without taking up valuable square footage.
- **Reflective Surfaces**: If your space allows, consider placing abstract art near mirrors or glossy surfaces to reflect

the artwork and multiply its impact. This can make the room feel larger and more dynamic, as the art appears in multiple places within the space.

- **Example**: In a small bathroom, hang an abstract artwork across from a large mirror. The reflection will double the visual impact of the art, making the room feel larger and more sophisticated.

- **Create Depth**: In compact areas, abstract art can be used to create the illusion of depth. Pieces that feature layered or textured elements can add dimension to flat walls, making the room feel more dynamic and expansive.

- **Example**: A textured abstract painting with deep layers of color and texture can add depth to a small entryway, making the space feel more substantial and engaging.

A tall, narrow painting gives a room the illusion of
height.

Utilizing Corners and Unused Spaces

Often, corners and other awkward spaces in small rooms go
underutilized. However, these areas offer an opportunity to
add abstract art in a way that transforms the space.

- **Corner Art Displays**: Don't shy away from using corners as mini art galleries. Hanging abstract pieces in
  corners can create a cozy, art-filled nook that draws attention to an otherwise neglected part of the room.

- ◦ **Example**: In a small bedroom, hang a pair of abstract paintings at a 90-degree angle in a corner, creating a unique visual effect that frames the space without encroaching on the main living area.
- **Floating Shelves**: Another option for small spaces is to use floating shelves to display abstract sculptures or framed artwork. Shelves allow you to create dimension on walls without taking up floor space, and they can add visual height to a room.

  - ◦ **Example**: In a small kitchen, place an abstract sculpture or two on a floating shelf. This not only adds an artistic touch but also maximizes the vertical space, making the kitchen feel more thoughtfully designed.

Multipurpose Art: When Function Meets Form

In small spaces, art can serve more than just an aesthetic purpose—it can also be functional. Consider using abstract art in ways that contribute to the functionality of the room.

- **Abstract Room Dividers**: In a small studio apartment or open-plan office, an abstract art piece can function as a room divider. Rather than using a traditional partition, a large abstract painting or a series of panels can visually separate areas while maintaining an open, airy feel.

  - ◦ **Example**: In a studio apartment, a large abstract canvas is suspended from the ceiling to divide the sleeping area from the living area. The art creates a visual barrier without fully enclosing the space, preserving the apartment's sense of openness.

- **Functional Art Pieces**: Sculptural abstract art can also be functional. For example, abstract wall hooks or shelving units can double as both decor and practical storage solutions.

  - **Example**: In a small entryway, a set of abstract wall hooks in a sculptural design serves as both an artistic feature and a practical place to hang coats and bags. This dual-purpose approach maximizes the space while adding a creative touch.

Final Thoughts: Embracing the Power of Abstract Art in Small Spaces

Small spaces may come with limitations, but abstract art offers boundless possibilities for enhancing these environments. By carefully selecting and placing abstract pieces, you can transform even the most compact rooms into vibrant, dynamic spaces full of personality and creativity. Whether you're adding a splash of color, creating depth and dimension, or using functional art to maximize your space, abstract art allows you to make a big impact in even the smallest of areas.

12

Unexpected Art

In the world of interior design, creativity knows no bounds. While artwork traditionally adorns our walls and serves as the centerpiece of a room, there is an emerging trend that dares to challenge conventions—placing abstract art in unexpected locations. By doing so, we can transform even the most mundane parts of our homes or offices into captivating canvases of creativity. In this chapter, we explore the delightful and surprising ways in which abstract art can be integrated into unexpected spaces, adding an element of intrigue and visual interest to your environment.

Redefining Conventional Boundaries

Art has long been confined to specific locations, such as walls, galleries, and feature areas in our homes. However, as design evolves, so do the possibilities for where art can live. Placing art in unconventional spaces not only redefines the boundaries of interior design but also allows for a deeper, more interactive relationship with your environment.

Abstract art, in particular, lends itself well to this approach because of its fluid and open-ended nature. Its bold colors, forms, and textures can enliven any space, making it a perfect choice for those looking to surprise and delight both themselves and their guests.

The Element of Surprise

The true beauty of placing abstract art in unexpected places lies in the element of surprise. When art appears in locations where it is least expected, it transforms the space from ordinary to extraordinary. This approach invites both residents and guests to engage with their surroundings in new and exciting ways, creating moments of visual discovery that elevate the ambiance.

These moments of surprise infuse energy into spaces that might otherwise be overlooked. By transforming functional areas into artistic showcases, you can redefine how you—and others—experience your home or workplace.

The Inside of Closets: Hidden Gems of Artistry

Closets are typically thought of as purely functional spaces used for storage, but with a little creativity, they can become unexpected galleries of abstract art. Whether it's a walk-in closet or a small hallway storage space, the interior walls of these hidden areas offer unique opportunities to display vibrant and dynamic artwork.

- **Walk-In Closets**: Spacious walk-in closets present a perfect canvas for bold, colorful abstract pieces. Imagine opening your closet doors to be greeted by a burst of creativity—art that transforms the mundane act of selecting an outfit into an inspiring experience.

  - **Example**: Picture a walk-in closet adorned with a large, vibrant abstract painting on the back wall. The artwork's swirling colors and energetic brushstrokes contrast with the orderly arrangement of clothes and accessories, creating a delightful juxtaposition of art and functionality. Each morning, this hidden masterpiece sets a positive and creative tone for your day.

- **Hidden Treasures in Smaller Closets**: Even smaller closets, such as those under the stairs or in hallways, can become hidden art galleries. When these spaces are opened, they reveal captivating artworks that surprise and intrigue guests.

  - **Example**: A linen closet in the hallway, typically used to store towels and bedding, conceals a hidden treasure—an abstract painting. When guests open the door, they are met with an unexpected work of art, sparking conversations and adding an element of whimsy to an otherwise ordinary space.

Spacious walk-in closets present a perfect canvas for bold,
colorful abstract pieces.

Pantry Doors: Bringing Art to Your Kitchen

The kitchen is often considered the heart of the home, and pantry doors—while functional—are rarely thought of as artistic opportunities. However, by incorporating abstract art into these spaces, you can add an unexpected creative touch to your kitchen or dining area.

- **Kitchen Surprises**: The inside surface of a pantry door can be adorned with an abstract painting, bringing an element of joy and creativity to your daily routines. Each time you reach for an ingredient or open the pantry for your morning coffee, you're met with a burst of color and artistic expression.

- **Example**: Imagine a pantry door in your kitchen featuring an abstract artwork inspired by the vibrant hues of fruits and vegetables. Every time you open the door, the bright and bold colors energize the space, making cooking and meal prep more enjoyable and inspiring.

- **Dining Room Drama**: If your dining area includes a separate pantry, consider using the pantry door as a canvas for an abstract masterpiece. The hidden art can add an element of sophistication and intrigue during dinner parties and gatherings.

- **Example**: In a formal dining room, the pantry door conceals a stunning abstract painting that complements the room's color scheme. When you reveal this hidden artwork to guests, it becomes a conversation starter, adding a touch of surprise and sophistication to your dining experience.

Ceiling Wonders: Elevating Your Perspective

Ceilings are often overlooked as potential canvases for art, but they offer a unique opportunity to add creativity and surprise to your space. Incorporating abstract art on the ceiling can transform your perspective, turning an ordinary room into an extraordinary experience.

- **Bedroom Elegance**: In a bedroom, abstract art on the ceiling can create a dreamlike atmosphere, inviting relaxation and tranquility. As you lay in bed, the artwork above transports you to a world of imagination and serenity.

  - **Example**: Visualize a bedroom with a soothing abstract painting of soft blue and white clouds on the ceiling. As you drift off to sleep, the artwork evokes the feeling of floating through a peaceful sky, enhancing your relaxation and contributing to a restful night's sleep.

- **Office Inspiration**: In a home office or study, abstract art on the ceiling can serve as a source of inspiration and creativity. By looking up, you are reminded of the endless possibilities that art can evoke, encouraging innovative thinking.

  - **Example**: Your home office features a ceiling adorned with a bold geometric abstract design. The dynamic shapes and energizing colors provide a constant source of motivation, making the ceiling not only a functional part of the room but also an inspiring focal point that drives creativity during work.

Unveiling the Unexpected: Embracing Creativity in New Spaces

Placing abstract art in unexpected places invites surprise and delight into your daily life. Whether it's a hidden gallery in a closet, a vibrant painting on a pantry door, or an inspiring design on the ceiling, these unconventional locations turn mundane spaces into captivating canvases for creativity.

- **Example**: In a cozy reading nook, the ceiling above features an abstract artwork that mimics a starry night sky. As you curl up with a book, the ceiling becomes a portal to another world, igniting your imagination and adding an extra layer of magic to your reading experience.

By placing art in these unexpected locations, you break free from traditional design conventions and transform your environment into a place of constant discovery. These hidden or unconventional artworks challenge the viewer to see the space in new ways, redefining their relationship with art and their surroundings.

The Joy of Discovery

There is something deeply satisfying about discovering art in unexpected places. It encourages us to look beyond the obvious and appreciate the details and creativity woven into the fabric of our daily lives. Whether it's a painting inside a closet or a mural on the ceiling, these surprising canvases enhance the atmosphere and create moments of joy and curiosity for both you and your guests.

So, when seeking to elevate your space with surprise and artistry, think beyond the traditional and explore the unexpected places where abstract art can reside. These hidden gems will not only transform your environment but also elevate your appreciation for the artistry that surrounds you.

13

Art in Outdoor Spaces

The great outdoors, with its boundless beauty and ever-changing landscapes, offers a unique and expansive canvas for creative expression. While we often think of art as something confined to the walls of our homes and workplaces, there's a growing trend toward incorporating art into outdoor environments. Whether it's a lush garden, a welcoming patio, or a cozy balcony, the fusion of nature and abstract art can transform these spaces into breathtaking sanctuaries of creativity. In this chapter, we'll explore how abstract art can thrive in outdoor settings, enhancing the natural world and turning gardens, patios, and balconies into stunning works of art.

Bringing Art to the Elements

Outdoor abstract art isn't just about aesthetics; it's about creating harmony between the elements and human creativity.

The beauty of outdoor art lies in its ability to complement and elevate the natural environment, while embracing the sun, wind, rain, and seasons. With the availability of weather-resistant materials, abstract art can now flourish in outdoor settings without losing its vibrancy or structural integrity. Here's how strategically placing outdoor abstract art can redefine and enhance your outdoor spaces.

Garden Enchantment: Blending Art with Nature

Gardens are already brimming with life and color, making them a perfect setting for abstract art to shine. By integrating artistic elements, you can enrich the garden experience and create a space that engages both the senses and the imagination.

- **Floral Companions**: In a garden filled with colorful flowers and verdant foliage, abstract art can harmonize with the natural landscape. Sculptures and weatherproof paintings nestled among the blooms add another layer of beauty, turning your garden into a living gallery.

  - **Example**: Imagine a rose garden enhanced by a series of abstract sculptures scattered throughout. Each sculpture reflects the organic curves and colors of the surrounding flowers, creating a dialogue between art and nature. As you wander through the garden, the interplay of vibrant blooms and dynamic sculptures invites you to pause, reflect, and appreciate the art of the natural world.

- **Pathway Pizzazz**: Garden pathways are often overlooked as opportunities for artistic expression, but they offer the perfect canvas for creativity. Abstract stepping stones or mosaic designs can transform a simple path into a sensory journey, making each step through your garden an exploration of art.

  - **Example**: As you stroll through your garden, mosaic stepping stones beneath your feet form an abstract pattern that shifts with every step. The design changes from floral-inspired motifs to geometric forms, guiding your walk with a sense of whimsy and wonder. These artistic elements add a touch of surprise and delight to your garden, making every journey through it feel like an adventure.

Patio Bliss: Transforming Outdoor Living Spaces

Patios are extensions of our homes, providing outdoor spaces for relaxation, socializing, and dining. By incorporating abstract art, you can elevate the ambiance of your patio, creating a space that is both stylish and inviting. The art becomes not just a decoration, but a conversation piece that adds depth to your outdoor sanctuary.

- **Focal Point**: A striking, weather-resistant abstract sculpture or painting can serve as the centerpiece of your patio, drawing attention and setting the tone for the space. These artworks anchor the design of your patio and offer a focal point around which conversations and gatherings revolve.

- **Example**: Picture a sleek, modern patio with a large abstract sculpture as its focal point. The sculpture's fluid lines and bold colors contrast with the natural materials of the patio furniture, creating a harmonious blend of modernity and nature. As guests gather for an outdoor dinner, the sculpture becomes a conversation starter, sparking discussions about art, design, and the beauty of the outdoor setting.

- **Vertical Gardens**: Vertical gardens, which combine greenery and abstract art, can turn an ordinary patio into a lush urban oasis. Weather-resistant abstract planters or artwork integrated into the vertical garden add texture and artistic flair, creating a living wall that merges nature and creativity.

  - **Example**: On your apartment balcony, a vertical garden featuring abstract planters filled with cascading vines transforms the space into a verdant sanctuary. The abstract design of the planters adds a modern touch, while the plants soften the space with organic beauty. This living art installation brings nature and abstraction together in a way that maximizes both space and style, offering a refreshing escape from the city.

An abstract painting becomes not just a decoration, but a conversation piece that adds depth to your outdoor sanctuary.

Balcony Retreat: Maximizing Small Outdoor Spaces

Balconies, while often small, offer a perfect opportunity to create a personal retreat where you can enjoy fresh air and quiet moments. Even the smallest of balconies can be transformed with the addition of abstract art, turning these intimate spaces into serene escapes filled with creativity.

• **Balcony Murals:** A weather-resistant abstract mural or

large painting can turn a blank balcony wall into a striking artistic statement. This not only elevates the aesthetics of your balcony but also creates a sense of expansion, making the space feel larger and more open.

- **Example:** Your city balcony overlooks the bustling skyline, but the walls remain bare and uninspired. By adding a vibrant abstract mural to one wall—perhaps a design that echoes the shapes and colors of the cityscape—you create a visual link between the urban environment and your personal retreat. The mural draws the eye outward, transforming your balcony into a dynamic and art-filled oasis.

- **Potted Art**: For those with limited space, potted abstract sculptures or decorative elements can add personality and style to a balcony without taking up much room. These small but impactful pieces can be nestled among potted plants or displayed on railings, adding a touch of creativity to your outdoor retreat.

  - **Example:** On your cozy balcony, abstract sculptures are placed among potted plants, each piece offering a unique contrast to the greenery. The sculptures' bold shapes and vibrant colors create a sense of playfulness and surprise, turning your small outdoor space into a serene escape filled with artistic expression.

Elevating Nature's Beauty: A Harmonious Fusion

The integration of abstract art into outdoor spaces is about more than decoration—it's about enhancing the natural beauty that surrounds you. By choosing weather-resistant art pieces that can withstand the elements, you create inviting outdoor sanctuaries that reflect your unique style and foster a deeper connection with nature.

- **Example**: In your garden, a series of tall abstract sculptures stand among the trees, their forms echoing the movement of the wind and the changing light of the seasons. As the sun sets, the sculptures cast long shadows, creating a dynamic interplay between art and nature. Each visit to your garden reveals something new—a subtle change in how the art interacts with the environment, inspiring awe and wonder in all who experience it.

This fusion of art and nature turns your outdoor spaces into living galleries, where both creativity and the natural world are celebrated.

Art that Adapts to Nature: Weather-Resistant Masterpieces

One of the key considerations when introducing art into outdoor spaces is durability. Outdoor abstract art needs to withstand exposure to the elements, from rain and wind to sunlight and temperature fluctuations. Fortunately, many artists now create weather-resistant masterpieces using materials such as metal, stone, and specially treated wood. These materials ensure that your outdoor art remains vibrant and intact, even in challenging weather conditions.

By investing in weather-resistant art, you not only enhance the longevity of your outdoor pieces but also maintain their visual appeal throughout the seasons. This ensures that your outdoor sanctuary remains an inviting and inspiring space year-round.

Unlocking the Full Potential of Outdoor Abstract Art

The possibilities for integrating abstract art into outdoor spaces are limited only by your imagination. Whether you have a sprawling garden, a compact patio, or a small balcony, abstract art can transform these spaces into places of beauty and contemplation. The key is to select pieces that complement the natural surroundings and reflect your personal style.

So, as you explore the potential of outdoor abstract art, remember that your gardens, patios, and balconies are more than just extensions of your home—they are canvases for creativity and expressions of your connection with the great outdoors. By bringing art into these spaces, you can elevate your outdoor living experience and create a harmonious fusion of nature and artistry that will inspire and delight you for years to come.

14

❧

Connecting Nature with Indoor Spaces

The boundary between outdoor and indoor spaces is often seen as rigid, but with thoughtful design, it can be blurred to create a seamless, harmonious flow. Abstract art can play a pivotal role in bridging this gap, connecting the organic beauty of the outdoors with the cultivated aesthetic of indoor environments. In this chapter, we explore how to use abstract art to create fluid transitions from outdoor to indoor spaces, enhancing the connection between nature and your home or office.

Creating a Seamless Flow Between Outdoors and Indoors

Transitioning from outdoor to indoor spaces is not just about design; it's about creating an experience that feels cohesive and connected. Abstract art can act as the perfect bridge, using natural forms, colors, and textures to draw the eye from the outdoor landscape into the interior.

- **Example**: In a home with a large garden, an abstract painting featuring earthy tones and organic, flowing shapes can be placed just inside the patio doors. This piece acts as a visual extension of the garden, softening the transition between the natural world and the home's interior.

Mirroring Natural Elements with Abstract Art

One of the most effective ways to connect outdoor and indoor spaces is by using abstract art that reflects the colors and forms of nature. Whether through sculptures, paintings, or textiles, abstract art can mimic the organic shapes and hues found outside, helping to create a sense of continuity between the two environments.

1. **Color Palette**
   Choose abstract art that echoes the colors of your outdoor landscape—whether that's the greenery of a garden, the blues of a swimming pool, or the earthy tones of a desert environment.

   - **Example**: A living room overlooking the ocean might feature abstract art in soft blues and greens, with wave-like patterns that mirror the movement and color of the water outside, creating a fluid connection between the seascape and the interior.

2. **Organic Shapes**
Abstract art often incorporates flowing, organic shapes that can evoke the curves of plants, trees, or natural formations. These shapes help integrate the indoor space with the outdoors, creating a sense of harmony.

- ○ **Example**: A sculpture with soft, rounded edges and natural materials, placed near a window with a view of the garden, can act as a continuation of the outdoor shapes, blurring the line between the natural and built environments.

3. **Textures and Materials**
Abstract art made from natural materials, such as wood, stone, or metal, can enhance the tactile connection between indoor and outdoor spaces. The use of these materials reflects the textures found in nature, helping to create a seamless transition.

- ○ **Example**: A metal wall sculpture featuring abstract leaf shapes in the entryway can act as a focal point that draws from the garden's foliage, reinforcing the connection between the two spaces.

A sculpture placed near a door or window with a view of
the garden can act as a continuation of the outdoor
shapes, blurring the line between the natural and built
environments.

Blurring Boundaries: Bringing the Outdoors In

One way to make the transition between outdoor and indoor
spaces feel more natural is by physically extending the outdoor
aesthetic into the home. Abstract art that complements the
natural elements in your yard, garden, or patio can create the
feeling of one continuous space.

- **Example**: In a home with large sliding glass doors, an

abstract mural on an interior wall can mirror the colors and patterns of the garden outside, creating the illusion that the garden extends into the house. The result is a space that feels open, unified, and in tune with nature.

Sculptural Installations for a Natural Flow

Sculptural installations can be particularly effective in creating an outdoor-to-indoor transition. By placing sculptures that resemble natural forms at key transition points—such as entryways, patios, or verandas—you can guide the flow of movement from the outside in, making the shift feel more organic.

- **Example**: A stone or metal sculpture with abstract, tree-like forms can be placed on a patio, where it serves as a transitional element. The same shapes can be echoed in smaller indoor sculptures, visually linking the two environments.

Seasonal Transitions: Adapting Art with Nature

As the seasons change, the colors and atmosphere of your outdoor space shift. By rotating your indoor abstract art to reflect these seasonal changes, you can further enhance the connection between the two environments and keep your space feeling fresh and attuned to nature.

- **Example**: In the spring and summer, bright, vibrant abstract paintings might fill the walls, echoing the lively colors of blooming flowers outside. In the fall and winter, you could switch to more muted, warm-toned pieces that reflect the earthier tones of the season.

Final Thoughts: Creating Harmony with Nature and Art

By thoughtfully integrating abstract art into your home or office, you can create a harmonious transition between outdoor and indoor spaces that feels cohesive, natural, and deeply connected to your surroundings. The result is an environment that fosters well-being and invites a deeper connection to both art and nature, elevating the aesthetic and emotional experience of your space.

15

Art Rotation

Imagine walking into a room and experiencing the thrill of encountering new art, even if you've been there countless times before. This is the transformative power of art rotation—an ingenious concept that breathes new life into your space, keeping it fresh, stimulating, and perpetually evolving. Whether in your home or office, regularly rotating art pieces invites a sense of discovery and allows you to engage with your collection in exciting new ways. In this chapter, we'll delve into how art rotation can enhance your connection with your collection and elevate the aesthetic energy of your environment.

The Beauty of Art Rotation

Art rotation is like having your own personal gallery within your space, offering an ever-changing visual experience that keeps things dynamic and engaging. Rather than letting your art collection remain static, art rotation allows you to curate new experiences with each change, encouraging exploration and a deeper appreciation of your collection.

Shifting Perspectives: Embracing Frequent Change

The core principle of art rotation is simple: regularly change the artworks on display. This rotation could be monthly, seasonally, or even annually, depending on your preferences and lifestyle. By shifting your art frequently, you infuse vibrancy into your space, transforming it into a living gallery where new narratives unfold with each change.

- **Example**: In your living room, you start with a bold abstract expressionist painting that features vibrant colors and dynamic brushstrokes. After a few months, you swap it out for a serene, nature-inspired piece that evokes a sense of calm and tranquility. This change alters the mood of the room, creating a fresh atmosphere that feels new and exciting.

Each time you rotate the art, you shift the energy and perspective of the space, offering yourself and your guests an ever-evolving visual experience.

Preventing Monotony: Endless Exploration of Your Collection

One of the greatest advantages of art rotation is that it prevents visual monotony. When art remains in the same place for too long, we can become so accustomed to it that it fades into the background. Art rotation keeps your environment dynamic, ensuring that your art continues to capture attention and inspire.

- **Example**: You have a collection of abstract art pieces, each with its own unique style and emotional resonance. By rotating them, you invite guests—and even yourself—to engage with these diverse expressions regularly. Each artwork offers something new to explore, preventing your space from becoming stale or predictable.

Rotation keeps your collection fresh and ensures that you never grow tired of the pieces that you've carefully curated over time.

Matching the Mood: Adapting Art to the Seasons

Art has the power to evoke specific moods and emotions, and by rotating your pieces to match the changing seasons or occasions, you can align the energy of your space with the time of year. This thoughtful approach allows you to create an environment that feels attuned to the rhythm of life.

- **Example**: In the spring, you display artworks with bright, lively colors that celebrate the season's vitality. As autumn and winter approach, you opt for art with warm tones and cozy themes, creating a snug, inviting atmosphere. This seasonal rotation keeps your space aligned with nature's transitions, bringing a sense of harmony and flow to your home.

By matching your art rotation to the seasons, you create a space that feels alive and responsive to the world around you. Rotating your collection based on seasonal shifts also ensures that your space remains engaging throughout the year.

Curating Experiences: The Power of Themed Exhibitions

Art rotation offers you the chance to become your own curator, creating mini-exhibitions within your space. By grouping artworks by theme, color, or artist, you can design curated experiences that invite deeper exploration and conversation.

- **Example**: You have a collection of landscape paintings. During one rotation, you decide to create an "Art in Nature" exhibit, displaying pieces that showcase the beauty of the natural world. This theme invites you and your guests to connect with nature through art, sparking conversations about the artists, the landscapes, and the emotions they evoke.

These curated experiences allow you to highlight different aspects of your collection, transforming your space into a gallery that reflects your artistic vision.

A Fresh Perspective: Renewed Appreciation for Your Art

Rotating your art ensures that you never become desensitized to the pieces you love. Each time you bring a familiar artwork back into the spotlight, it's like reuniting with an old friend. You see it with fresh eyes, and its beauty and meaning are renewed.

- **Example**: An abstract sculpture in your office's entrance was initially a conversation starter with clients. After a few rotations, you bring it back, and it feels as though you're rediscovering its charm. It becomes a cherished piece that sparks a sense of nostalgia each time you pass by, reawakening your connection to it.

Art rotation keeps your relationship with your collection alive and evolving, ensuring that each piece remains a source of inspiration.

Simple Guidelines for Art Rotation: Practical Considerations

While art rotation is an exciting and creative process, it's important to follow some practical guidelines to protect your art during its downtime. Proper storage is key to ensuring that the pieces not currently on display remain in pristine condition.

- **Example**: You invest in specialized art racks and protective covers to safely store the artworks that are not currently on display. These storage solutions ensure that your collection is well-maintained and ready to be rotated back into your space whenever the time comes.

Taking care of your collection with proper storage is essential for maintaining the longevity and value of your artworks.

Unleash Your Creativity: Experiment and Discover

Art rotation encourages experimentation—an opportunity to play with new arrangements, combinations, and themes. By rotating art, you can discover unique visual narratives and interactions within your space, finding new ways to appreciate the pieces you love.

- **Example**: You decide to create a themed wall in your dining room, featuring rotating artworks that reflect your culinary adventures. As you experiment with different art pieces—perhaps a series inspired by food or nature—you uncover new ways to celebrate your love for both food and art. Each rotation brings a new layer of creativity to your dining experience.

This freedom to experiment allows you to continuously reinvent your space, keeping it vibrant and full of surprises.

Rotating your art enables you to rearrange pieces
according to themes.

A Living Canvas: Your Space in Constant Evolution

When you embrace art rotation, you begin to view your space as a living canvas—an environment that is ever-evolving and reflective of your taste, interests, and emotions. Your home or office becomes a place of artistic exploration, where the stories of your collection are always in motion.

- **Example**: Your friends eagerly anticipate visiting your home, knowing that each time they come, they'll be greeted by a fresh, artistic narrative. The art rotation has transformed your space into a dynamic gallery where no two visits are ever the same, and every room offers a new perspective on your artistic journey.

Art rotation keeps your space alive, reflecting your growth and evolving relationship with the pieces you love.

Embrace the Transformation: An Evolving Connection

Art rotation is more than just changing the décor—it's about building an evolving connection with your art collection. It invites you to embrace the transformation of your space, forging deeper relationships with each piece as it comes back into view.

- **Example**: Over time, your art rotation ritual becomes a cherished part of your life. It's a moment of reflection and creativity, where you curate your environment to match your current mood or phase in life. The process keeps your space in perpetual motion, mirroring the ever-changing landscape of your thoughts, emotions, and experiences.

Art rotation brings meaning and intentionality to your space, transforming it into a living reflection of who you are.

Endless Exploration Awaits: The Unlimited Potential of Art Rotation

The potential for art rotation is limitless. As your art collection grows, each new addition brings with it the possibility to redefine your space in exciting ways. By continuously rotating your art, you ensure that every piece gets its moment in the spotlight, offering new perspectives and discoveries with each change.

- **Example:** Over the years, your art collection expands, and each new piece offers the opportunity to refresh your environment. With each rotation, you find new ways to appreciate and interact with the art, allowing your space to grow and evolve alongside your collection.

Art rotation invites you to embark on a journey of endless exploration, where each change brings new beauty, inspiration, and meaning.

16

Sound and Art Fusion

Imagine stepping into a room where not only your eyes but also your ears are greeted with artistry. This is the enchanting world of sound and art fusion—a realm where visual and auditory experiences intertwine to create something truly magical. When art and sound come together, they offer a multisensory journey that deepens your connection to the creative universe and transforms your space into an immersive experience. In this chapter, we'll explore how sound and art can harmoniously coexist, offering endless possibilities for creating an environment that stimulates both the eyes and ears.

The concept of sound and art fusion brings together two powerful senses—sight and hearing.

The Fusion of Art and Sound

The concept of sound and art fusion brings together two powerful senses—sight and hearing—creating a rich, dynamic layer of creativity and sensory delight. By integrating sound with visual art, you open the door to new ways of experiencing and interacting with your surroundings. Here's how this fusion can transform your space.

Synchronized Illumination: Art that Reacts to Sound

One of the most exciting ways to combine sound and art is through sound-responsive lighting systems. These innovative systems allow your abstract art pieces to visually respond to the sounds in their environment, creating an immersive experience where the artwork's appearance evolves in harmony with the surrounding soundscape. As the sound changes, so does the art.

- **Example**: You have a vibrant abstract painting featuring bold strokes and dynamic colors. By pairing it with sound-responsive lighting, the colors of the artwork can shift and pulsate in rhythm with music or ambient noise. Imagine hosting a gathering where the art itself becomes a living, breathing part of the musical experience. The lights dance in sync with the beats of the music, turning your artwork into an ever-changing spectacle.

This synchronized illumination adds a dynamic element to your space, creating an interplay between art, light, and sound that enhances the emotional impact of both the artwork and the music.

Interactive Soundscapes: Becoming Part of the Art

Auditory art installations invite you to step inside the art itself, where you can interact with sounds and visuals in a way that blurs the line between observer and participant. These immersive experiences turn you into an active part of the artwork, allowing you to engage with sound and art on a deeper level.

- **Example**: You enter an installation featuring an abstract sculpture. As you move around the sculpture, sensors detect your presence and trigger a symphony of sounds that correspond to different elements of the artwork. Your movements become a dance of sound and light, with the sculpture responding to your presence and creating a unique auditory and visual experience. This fusion of sound and art transforms the traditional viewing experience, making you an integral part of the creative process.

Interactive soundscapes encourage exploration, inviting you to engage with the art in ways that transcend traditional boundaries.

Musical Paintings: Composing with Colors

Some artists are exploring the concept of musical paintings, where visual art is created directly in response to music. These artworks are born from the emotional and auditory experience of listening to specific compositions, translating the rhythms, melodies, and dynamics of music into a visual form.

- **Example**: An artist listens to a classical composition and uses it as inspiration for an abstract painting. The flow of the brush, the choice of colors, and the arrangement of shapes are all influenced by the music's tempo, mood, and emotional range. The resulting painting becomes a visual representation of the musical journey, allowing viewers to experience the music through the artist's interpretation.

Musical paintings merge two art forms, offering a visual manifestation of music's emotional and dynamic power, and inviting viewers to explore the connection between sight and sound.

Innovative Technologies: Exploring Art Through Digital Soundscapes

Advancements in technology have given rise to interactive art experiences through augmented reality (AR) and virtual reality (VR). These technologies allow you to engage with art in new ways by merging digital soundscapes with visual elements, creating immersive environments that go beyond traditional art viewing.

- **Example**: You download an AR app and point your smartphone at an abstract painting in your home. Suddenly, the artwork comes to life with accompanying sounds that match the different elements of the painting. The colors evoke soothing tones, while the sharper, more angular parts of the artwork emit higher-pitched sounds. You can even interact with the painting by "painting" your own sounds onto the canvas using the app, creating a personalized auditory experience.

Interactive technologies like AR and VR provide a bridge between the physical and digital worlds, allowing you to explore the fusion of sound and art in new and exciting ways.

Customized Compositions: Bespoke Soundscapes for Your Art

For a truly personalized multisensory experience, consider commissioning bespoke soundscapes for your art collection. Collaborating with a composer to create musical compositions tailored to specific artworks can add an extra layer of emotional depth and meaning to your collection.

- **Example**: You own a collection of abstract paintings, each with a unique style and mood. You work with a composer to create a series of musical compositions—one for each painting. When you or your guests view the art, you play the corresponding composition, allowing the music to enhance the emotional resonance of the piece. This creates a multisensory experience that deepens the connection between the viewer and the art.

Customized soundscapes offer an unparalleled level of personalization, turning your art collection into a symphony of sight and sound.

The Symbiosis of Senses: A Harmonious Connection

The fusion of sound and art isn't just about creating a sensory spectacle—it's about forging a profound connection between the visual and auditory senses. When these two art forms come together, they elevate each other, creating a richer and more immersive experience that engages the viewer on multiple levels.

- **Example**: In your home, you have a collection of abstract art pieces, each paired with a specific musical composition. As you move from one artwork to the next, you listen to the corresponding soundscape, immersing yourself in a multisensory journey that awakens your senses and stirs your emotions. This fusion of sight and sound creates a deeper, more meaningful connection to the art.

By engaging multiple senses simultaneously, sound and art fusion invites you to explore the full spectrum of sensory perception, transforming the way you experience art.

Embrace the Symphony: A Feast for the Senses

Sound and art fusion offers endless opportunities for creativity. It challenges traditional boundaries and invites you to explore the limitless possibilities of human expression. By embracing this fusion, you turn your space into a canvas where colors, shapes, and sounds interact in harmony.

- **Example**: You attend an art exhibition where the artworks respond to the music playing in the background. As you walk through the gallery, you witness a symphony of colors, shapes, and sounds, each piece telling a unique story through this multisensory narrative. The entire space feels alive, with each artwork and sound working together to create an immersive experience.

This integration of art and sound transforms your environment into a living gallery, where every sense is engaged in the creative process.

A Living Symphony: Your Space as a Multisensory Experience

By embracing sound and art fusion, you immerse yourself in a rich tapestry of sensory experiences. Your space becomes a **living symphony**, where colors dance to the rhythm of sound, and each artwork invites you to see, hear, and feel the world in a new way.

- **Example**: You create a dedicated sound and art room in your home. Inside, you display your most cherished abstract pieces, and the room is equipped with state-of-the-art sound technology. As you view each artwork, you choose a corresponding soundtrack to accompany it, allowing you to fully immerse yourself in the fusion of sight and sound.

This multisensory space becomes a place of inspiration and creativity, offering endless possibilities for artistic exploration.

17

Interactive Abstract Art

Abstract art isn't just something to be admired from afar—it can also be an immersive, tactile experience that invites viewers to engage directly with the piece. By creating or incorporating interactive abstract art into your home or office, you can transform static environments into dynamic, engaging spaces. In this chapter, we'll explore how interactive abstract art can become a playful, functional, and visually stimulating element in your surroundings, encouraging creativity and connection.

The Concept of Interactivity in Abstract Art

Interactive abstract art allows viewers to become participants rather than passive observers. Whether through touch, movement, or even sound, these artworks can change and evolve based on human interaction, offering a more personal and immersive experience.

- **Example**: Imagine a large, modular abstract art installation in an open office space. Each piece can be rearranged to create new compositions, allowing employees to collaborate on the design or refresh the aesthetic of their environment regularly. This fosters a sense of ownership and connection with the space.

By breaking down the barrier between viewer and art, interactive pieces invite a deeper level of engagement, making the experience of living or working with art more dynamic and personal.

Interactive abstract art allows viewers to become participants rather than passive observers.

Types of Interactive Abstract Art

There are several types of interactive abstract art that can be incorporated into home or office spaces, each offering a unique way to engage with the artwork:

1. **Modular Art Pieces**
   Modular abstract art consists of components that can be rearranged to form different compositions. This type of art is perfect for those who like to change their decor

frequently or for spaces that need to accommodate different functions.

- ◦ **Example**: A wall installation made up of individual abstract tiles that can be rotated or swapped around allows you to change the look of the piece whenever you like. This flexibility adds a playful, ever-changing dynamic to a room.

2. **Tactile Art**

Tactile abstract art invites viewers to touch or physically interact with the artwork. Textured paintings, sculptures with moveable parts, or soft fabric-based art pieces encourage people to engage with their sense of touch, making the artwork a multisensory experience.

- ◦ **Example**: In a living room, a large abstract tapestry with various textures—smooth silk, rough wool, soft velvet—can be displayed on a wall or used as a floor piece. Guests are encouraged to touch and feel the different materials, creating a richer sensory experience.

3. **Interactive Sculptures**

Interactive sculptures offer a more three-dimensional experience, allowing people to move around or manipulate the piece. These sculptures can be kinetic (moving with the touch of a hand or wind) or designed to change shape when interacted with.

- ◦ **Example**: A sculptural piece in a communal office space might feature interconnected panels that rotate on axes. Employees can adjust the panels throughout the day, creating different shapes and compositions. This introduces an element of play into the workplace, fostering creativity and collaboration.

4. **Light-Responsive Art**

Light plays a significant role in how we perceive abstract art, and light-responsive art takes this relationship to a new level. These pieces are designed to react to changes in light, whether through natural sunlight, artificial lighting, or even changes in brightness as people move through a room.

- ○ **Example**: In a hallway, an abstract glass sculpture catches sunlight streaming through the windows, casting colorful shadows that shift throughout the day. The play of light on the artwork creates an evolving visual experience that changes with the time of day and season.

5. **Sound-Interactive Art**

Some interactive abstract art incorporates sound as part of the experience. These pieces might produce sound when touched, or they might change based on ambient noise in the environment. Sound-interactive art adds a new dimension to spaces, stimulating both sight and hearing.

- ○ **Example**: In a creative office space, a large abstract wall installation made of suspended metal shapes creates soft chimes as people walk past. The interaction with the piece becomes part of the office's soundscape, blending art with the everyday activity of the workspace.

Designing Interactive Art Spaces

Incorporating interactive abstract art into your home or office requires thoughtful consideration of how people will engage with the space. Here are some tips for designing spaces around interactive art:

- **Create Open, Accessible Areas**: Interactive art requires space for people to move and engage. Ensure that there's enough room around the artwork for interaction without disrupting the flow of the room.

    - **Example**: In an open-plan office, an interactive art installation in the break area can encourage employees to engage with the art during their downtime, providing both a creative outlet and a focal point for relaxation.

- **Encourage Playfulness**: Interactive art thrives in spaces where people feel free to explore and experiment. Use bright colors, tactile materials, and unusual shapes to create an inviting atmosphere.

    - **Example**: In a children's playroom, an abstract art piece made from soft, colorful blocks can double as both a decorative wall feature and a hands-on activity, allowing children to build, rearrange, and interact with the artwork.

- **Integrate Art with Functionality**: In addition to being visually engaging, interactive art can also serve practical purposes. It can double as a room divider, lighting fixture, or even storage.

  - **Example**: A rotating abstract art panel in a small home office can serve as both art and a room divider, separating work and living spaces in a creative, flexible way.

- **Use Technology to Enhance Interactivity**: Advances in technology have expanded the possibilities for interactive art. Pieces that respond to movement, sound, or touch through sensors and LED lighting can create a highly immersive experience.

  - **Example**: In a modern living room, an interactive LED abstract painting responds to the presence of people, subtly changing color and brightness as someone walks by, creating a personalized, everchanging environment.

The Emotional Impact of Interactive Art

One of the most significant benefits of interactive abstract art is its ability to engage people on an emotional level. By inviting viewers to become part of the creative process, interactive art fosters a deeper connection with the artwork and the space it inhabits. This sense of participation can create lasting memories and make a room feel more alive and engaging.

- **Example**: A couple installs an interactive abstract sculpture in their entryway. The sculpture responds to touch, lighting up with different colors depending on where it's touched. Over time, it becomes a daily ritual to interact with the art as they come home, creating a sense of joy and playfulness that elevates their daily routine.

Final Thoughts: Bringing Life to Your Space with Interactive Abstract Art

Interactive abstract art transforms the way we experience and engage with our surroundings. By inviting touch, movement, or sound, these pieces blur the line between art and environment, making the viewer an active participant in the creative process. Whether in a home, office, or public space, interactive abstract art adds depth, energy, and a sense of playfulness that enhances both the aesthetic and emotional qualities of the room.

As you explore the world of interactive art, consider how these dynamic pieces can transform your living and working spaces into places of connection, creativity, and engagement. Interactive art not only enriches the visual experience but also deepens the emotional impact, turning every interaction into a new opportunity for discovery.

18

Art for Branding

In the modern corporate world, the fusion of art and business has become a powerful tool for expressing a company's ethos, character, and culture. Abstract art, with its ability to evoke emotions, transcend traditional boundaries, and spark creativity, offers a unique opportunity to reinforce a company's branding.

By strategically incorporating abstract art into corporate spaces, businesses can create environments that reflect their values, inspire employees, and leave a lasting impression on clients and stakeholders. In this chapter, we'll explore the strategic use of abstract art in corporate branding and how it can become an integral part of a company's identity.

The Business of Art: Aesthetic Signatures for Corporate Spaces

Just as a company's logo serves as its visual signature, abstract art can become an aesthetic signature of the brand. The art that adorns a company's offices and client-facing spaces plays a crucial role in setting the tone for the business, communicating its values and vision in a visually engaging way.

- **Example**: A cutting-edge tech company known for innovation and creativity selects abstract art with bold, dynamic shapes and vibrant colors to decorate its office spaces. The art aligns with the company's brand values and visually communicates its commitment to forward-thinking solutions. Visitors entering the office are immediately greeted by the striking visual display, reinforcing the company's identity before any words are exchanged.

By integrating abstract art that complements the company's branding, businesses can create a cohesive and memorable aesthetic that enhances their corporate image.

Visual Storytelling: Reflecting the Company's Journey and Values

Abstract art has the power to tell a visual story. Companies can strategically select or commission artworks that reflect their journey, core values, or aspirations. These pieces become more than decoration—they serve as a visual narrative that sparks conversations and offers insights into the company's culture.

- **Example**: An environmentally conscious company commissions an abstract art installation that incorporates recycled materials. The artwork serves as a symbol of the company's commitment to sustainability and sparks conversations about its eco-friendly initiatives. Clients and employees alike are reminded of the company's values each time they encounter the artwork, creating a strong, lasting connection between the brand and its environmental mission.

Incorporating abstract art that resonates with the company's story helps communicate its vision and values in a subtle yet impactful way, enhancing both internal culture and external perception.

Creating a Branded Experience: Client Engagement and Employee Motivation

First impressions are vital in business, and the design of client-facing areas is crucial for creating a positive experience. Abstract art can transform corporate lobbies, meeting rooms, and waiting areas into spaces that are welcoming, inspiring, and aligned with the company's identity.

- **Example**: A law firm that specializes in intellectual property showcases abstract art in its reception area. The art, which features modern and inventive designs, speaks to the firm's expertise in the creative industries. The artwork not only enhances the aesthetic appeal of the space but also subtly reinforces the firm's focus on creativity and innovation. Clients entering the firm's offices are immersed in an environment that reflects the firm's core strengths.

Abstract art also has a powerful role to play in boosting employee morale. By displaying art that resonates with the company's values and culture, businesses can foster a sense of belonging and pride among employees.

- **Example**: A healthcare organization commissions abstract art pieces that reflect its mission of wellness, empathy, and care. These pieces are strategically placed throughout the office, serving as daily reminders to employees of the organization's values. The presence of this art creates a positive and purposeful work environment, reinforcing the company's commitment to its mission.

In both client-facing and employee-centered spaces, abstract art becomes a tool for creating environments that reflect the company's culture and enhance engagement.

Reflecting Company Values: Diversity, Inclusion, and Innovation

Abstract art's inherent diversity of forms, interpretations, and perspectives makes it an ideal medium for mirroring a company's commitment to diversity and inclusion. By curating or commissioning artworks that celebrate different cultures and viewpoints, businesses can create inclusive environments that reflect their global or multicultural values.

- **Example**: A multinational corporation features a diverse collection of abstract art from artists around the world in its headquarters. This global approach to art curation highlights the company's dedication to inclusivity and the celebration of diverse perspectives. Employees and visitors are immersed in a culturally rich environment that aligns with the company's commitment to fostering an inclusive workplace.

Similarly, abstract art often embodies innovation and

creativity, making it a natural fit for companies that prioritize forward-thinking approaches and creative problem-solving.

- **Example**: A research and development company decorates its innovation hub with abstract art installations that inspire creative thinking and push boundaries. These installations become a source of inspiration for teams working on cutting-edge projects, encouraging them to think beyond conventional limits.

By integrating abstract art that reflects values of inclusivity, creativity, and innovation, companies can visually reinforce the principles that drive their success.

Customized Art: Tailored Expressions of Brand Identity

One of the most powerful ways to integrate abstract art into corporate branding is through customized art commissions. By collaborating with artists, companies can create bespoke pieces that encapsulate their brand's identity, values, and vision. These artworks become one-of-a-kind expressions of the company's ethos.

- **Example**: An architecture firm working on sustainable urban development commissions a series of abstract art pieces that reflect the firm's vision for vibrant, eco-friendly cityscapes. These artworks are displayed in the firm's lobby and conference rooms, serving as visual representations of the company's dedication to sustainable design. Each piece becomes a talking point for clients and stakeholders, reinforcing the firm's core values.

Customized art allows businesses to create a unique aesthetic signature that speaks directly to their brand's narrative.

Enhancing Productivity and Collaboration: The Role of Art in the Workplace

Abstract art can play a functional role in the workplace, promoting **productivity** and **focus** through its use of color, form, and design. Geometric abstract patterns, for example, can enhance mental clarity and concentration, while more fluid, organic designs can inspire creativity and collaboration.

- **Example**: An accounting firm decorates its conference rooms with abstract art that features clean, geometric shapes. The art's structure and precision mirror the focus required for the firm's work, promoting a professional atmosphere while subtly encouraging productivity.

In collaborative spaces, abstract art can serve as a catalyst for brainstorming and teamwork. Art that invites interaction or discussion can invigorate these environments, fostering creativity and dynamic exchange.

- **Example**: A marketing agency designs its creative brainstorming room with interactive abstract art pieces that encourage team members to engage with the art. These installations become a source of spontaneous conversation and inspiration during team meetings, driving innovative thinking and collaboration.

In both individual workspaces and collaborative settings, abstract art can enhance the office environment by promoting focus, creativity, and a sense of shared purpose.

Brand Integration and Beyond: Extending the Impact of Abstract Art

The influence of abstract art can extend beyond the physical office space, becoming an integral part of a company's marketing materials, website design, and social media presence. By incorporating abstract art into these platforms, businesses can create a cohesive brand identity that resonates across all channels.

- **Example**: A fashion retailer integrates abstract art inspired by its seasonal collections into its marketing campaigns. The art appears on store displays, the company's website, and social media platforms, creating a unified and visually engaging brand narrative that connects with customers across all touchpoints.

Similarly, abstract art can play a central role in corporate events, product launches, and conferences. Customized art installations designed specifically for these occasions can highlight the event's theme or message, leaving a lasting impression on attendees.

- **Example**: A technology company hosts a product

launch event and commissions an abstract art installation that reflects the product's innovative features. The art becomes a focal point of the event, reinforcing the company's message of innovation and excellence.

By integrating abstract art into every aspect of the brand experience, companies can create a consistent, impactful identity that resonates with clients, employees, and stakeholders alike.

The Art of Success: Building a Corporate Identity Through Abstract Art

In the world of business, abstract art is more than just a visual element—it's a strategic tool for **branding** and **cultural expression**. Whether through curated art collections or bespoke commissions, abstract art has the power to convey a company's values, inspire employees, and leave a lasting impression on clients and visitors. By embracing the potential of abstract art, companies can create spaces that not only reflect their identity but also elevate their brand to new heights of success.

About the Author

Evan Stuart Marshall is an award-winning mixed-media ab-stract artist, celebrated for his quirky, playful, and whim-sical style. Originally from Boston and raised in Sharon, Massachusetts, he now lives and works in Roseland, New Jersey.

A largely self-taught artist, Evan has earned numerous acco-lades for his vibrant, distinctive paintings, which have been featured in solo and group exhibitions worldwide. His work, inspired by his love of color and texture, is held in private col-lections across the globe. His art is available through major on-line retailers including 1stDibs, Artsy, Wayfair, and Walmart, among others.

In addition to *Building Your Art Business*, Evan is the

author of *Abstract Art Revolution* and *Collecting Abstract Art on a Budget.*

Visit Evan's website at www.evanstuartmarshall.com.

Stay connected and follow his artistic journey on social media!

Facebook: facebook.com/evanstuartmarshall
Instagram: instagram.com/evanstuartmarshall
YouTube: youtube.com/evanstuartmarshallabstractart
Pinterest: pinterest.com/evanstuartmarshallart
X (formerly Twitter): x.com/esmarshallart

Stay Connected and Share Your Feedback

As an independent author, your support means the world to me! Your feedback not only helps me continue creating and sharing valuable content with artists like you, but it also helps other readers discover my work. If you found this book helpful or inspiring, I'd be incredibly grateful if you could take a moment to follow me and leave a rating or review on your favorite platform.

- Amazon Author Central: **https://t.ly/ASBBJ** – Discover my latest books and updates.
- BookBub: **https://t.ly/sIjDG** – Get notified about new releases and special offers.
- Goodreads: **https://t.ly/VuqQy** – Connect with me and join in on book discussions.
- IndieBound: **https://t.ly/nqxOz** – Support independent bookstores while leaving feedback.

www.ingramcontent.com/pod-product-compliance
Lightning Source LLC
Chambersburg PA
CBHW052032150726